MAKE YOUR SENSITIVITY

CW00689288

ALICE MUIR is an experienced
chologist and Life Coach. She is n.........
family. Alice is the youngest of eight children, and spent
her childhood in the Ayrshire countryside, before training
at Glasgow and Stirling Universities. She is a member of
the British Psychological Society, the General Teaching
Council, the International Stress Management Association
and the Association for Coaching. Alice has a long-
standing interest in personal development, and has been
writing and training on the subject, as well as coaching
groups and individuals, for the past 25 years. With Dr
Kenneth Hambly, she wrote *Coping with a Stressed
Nervous System*, also published by Sheldon Press.

Overcoming Common Problems Series

Selected titles

A full list of titles is available from Sheldon Press,
36 Causton Street, London SW1P 4ST and on our website at
www.sheldonpress.co.uk

Overcoming Common Problems

Make Your Sensitivity Work for You

Alice Muir

First published in Great Britain in 2006

Sheldon Press
36 Causton Street
London SW1P 4ST

British Library Cataloguing-in-Publication Data

A catalogue record for this book is available from the British Library

ISBN-13: 978–0–85969–973–0
ISBN-10: 0–85969–973–0

1 3 5 7 9 10 8 6 4 2

Typeset by Deltatype Limited, Birkenhead, Merseyside
Printed in Great Britain by Ashford Colour Press

For my inspirational and remarkable parents,
Margaret and Alexander McKie

Contents

Introduction

If you are reading this book, or thumbing through it in a bookshop, the chances are that you think that you are too sensitive. What makes you think this? What sorts of experiences have you had which have made you wonder about it, and moreover, want to do something about it? And why today? Why have you lifted this book up today, or bought it and taken it home with you? There is often a straw that has broken the camel's back and decided you that today, you must do something. You're sure that there has to be something you can do about this.

Perhaps you feel you've been let down one time too many, or that you spend too much time worrying about others' welfare rather than your own. Maybe you've fallen out with your best friend, or had yet another blazing row with your partner. Or maybe you just can't face another day with that loud-mouthed colleague at work, or have absolutely no idea how you're going to manage another day living next door to that difficult neighbour. Or maybe it's just like the dripping tap that goes on and on, and today, you are worn out and can't take any more of it. In other words, for whatever reason, your stress levels are just too high. Whatever it is, whatever has motivated you to do something, rest assured that this book will be able to help you.

Today probably lies at the end of many, many days of having problems with being too sensitive. You've probably been told many times that 'You're too sensitive for your own good.' If you've heard this one before, it doesn't mean you are a social outcast, mad, or doomed to failure – just that you view life differently to many people. Not worse, not better, just differently.

In this book, I'll show you that you shouldn't be wishing your sensitivity away. I'll show you that you should be proud of being sensitive. Being a sensitive person can be a really good thing too – there's another side to every coin. A sensitive person may well have more empathy and sympathy, more time for others – a sensitive person is often very well loved. A sensitive person may have a special role to play in life, such as taking on work in a charity or with animals, that demands an exceptional level of responsiveness.

This is a new start for you. This book will help you to cope better with the downside and frustrations of being sensitive – the hurt, guilt, and anxiety. I will help you to deal with situations more effectively, so that you can feel better, and be more relaxed, less moody, and happy with who you are. I'll explain how to feel and act more confidently, how to feel stronger and more in control of your life, and how simple tips about the way you think can transform your life for ever.

1

Are you too sensitive?

Do you seem to worry about what you're saying and doing all the time? Are you always concerned about others' reactions, and perhaps too eager to please? Making decisions can be a nightmare as you are so desperate to make sure that you get it right and don't upset anyone. If someone or something upsets you, you find you can't get it out of your mind. Do you often feel hurt or offended at a chance remark or by a friend's behaviour? Your sleep can be disturbed, with vivid or repetitive dreams, or you can be plagued by frighteningly realistic nightmares.

All this can make you tense, nervous, guilty, depressed, moody, with a poor self-image, and low self-esteem. You may even begin to hate yourself. This is such a tense, tiring, draining and frustrating way to live. It makes you perform less well in all areas of life, it damages relationships, and makes being a parent more difficult. It makes it so very difficult to make friends and keep them, to find and keep a partner – or just to have a quiet drink with someone.

Getting in touch with your sensitivity

If any of the following apply to you, reading this book is a must. You:

- feel you have a 'thin skin'
- are easily hurt
- are too touchy
- tend to over-react
- are easily offended
- are scared to offend other people
- are too eager to please
- don't like to be the centre of attention
- often feel guilty
- are easily flustered
- care too much what other people think
- can't take or give criticism
- worry all the time that you're saying, or have said the wrong thing
- are scared to say 'no' in case you offend someone

1

- feel someone who disagrees with you must dislike you
- think too much
- can't get things people have said out of your head
- feel you lack confidence and self-esteem
- often feel your nerves are on edge
- often feel life is frustrating
- always feel you could be doing better
- sometimes feel that life is passing you by
- have problems with your mood
- can be too emotional
- often sleep poorly

You feel you have a 'thin skin'

Do you feel different from most other people? Does everyone else seem to be stronger than you, with a 'thicker skin'? Other people seem to be able to just shrug things off, and move on – for example, if their boss pulls them up for being late or for not finishing a report on time. Or if a friend said she'd call and didn't, or if a neighbour complains about your dog barking. For many, it seems to be water off a duck's back. Why can't you be like that?

For you, it's different. You can't get such incidents out of your head for the rest of the day. You feel small and upset, and can't find a way to resolve the feelings. When you meet up later with your partner or a friend, you just want to offload all those feelings, but just succeed in upsetting him or her too. You collapse into bed at the end of the day, but can't get to sleep for going over and over it all in your head, then eventually fall into a fitful sleep, disturbed by dreams where you constantly replay the events of the day. Does any of this strike a chord with you?

You're easily hurt

Have you spent many an hour feeling hurt and upset about something someone said, or didn't say, to you? Or because someone forgot your birthday, or didn't congratulate you on some achievement? Or maybe a friend, whom you thought was a good friend, met you in town but didn't have time to talk, and rushed off. When someone appears not to have time for you, it hurts. You don't know what to say to your friend the next time you see him or her and may take steps to avoid another meeting; or, perhaps fall into an argument with your partner or closer friends. How exhausting it all is, and how much time it wastes.

Too touchy

All can be going along well, when a colleague at work says the wrong thing. 'I wouldn't have done that that way', or 'Haven't you organized that meeting yet?' The annoyance rises, and you don't know what to do with it. Or your neighbour has parked across your driveway and you can't get your car out to go to the shops. Your partner innocently asks if you've remembered to pay the electricity bill. Of course you have – does he think you're stupid? It's not just that you're touchy and easily set off – more that you tend to over-react and be angrier, sadder or more frustrated than is really appropriate.

Easily offended

Taking offence is the next step on from being hurt, a feeling which can last for a long time. Some people even lose friends or family this way – the feeling of being offended persists, and they can't feel the same way about the friend any more. This can extend to more personal relationships too, making it really difficult to sustain a relationship and keep a partner for long.

Scared to offend

Because you are easily offended, you assume that everybody else must be the same, so you take pains to ensure that you don't offend anyone either. You're just so eager to please everyone. This makes every day difficult, as you weigh up every situation that arises. Whom to ask to a party or outing. Remembering to send a card to everyone who gets engaged or passes a driving test, or has a baby. Making sure that your present is as good as the one they gave you. And of course, being scared to say 'no' to any request! It doesn't matter that you are tired and overloaded. You can't possibly let some-one down. After all, their needs are more important than yours – aren't they?

Often feel guilty

Mixed into all these situations is a tendency to feel guilty. Did you offend your mother when you didn't ask her to come for Christmas dinner this year? What about your friend who just got her degree? You forgot to send her a card. How terrible of you. At work, you're not on target for this month's sales. At home, you didn't get time to cut back that plant the neighbour complained to you about. How bad you feel. Life can feel like one endless guilt trip.

Care too much what other people think

Do you dress to please yourself, or to please others? Think about it. When you decide what to wear in the morning, whom are you thinking about? Is it you or is it your partner, or other people at the office? Some people won't even pop round to the corner shop without their make-up on and their hair done. Do you shrink from taking something back to a shop in case they make a fuss and people look at you, or in case the shop assistant is annoyed with you or refuses to take the item back? How many things do you have in your cupboards that you should have taken back or made a complaint about? And what about the bigger things in life: the job you do, the car you drive, or your home? Do you wonder endlessly what other people are thinking, and base your decisions on this? Maybe we should think more about the words of George Bernard Shaw, who said, 'Do not do unto others as you would they should do unto you. Their tastes may not be the same.'

Can't take or give criticism

You wish it weren't so, but you find even the smallest of criticisms hurts. It's a hurt that goes deep inside you, making you doubt yourself and your abilities. Doing even one small thing wrong or badly defines the whole of you. Anything less than perfection is not acceptable. This makes no more sense than saying that one weed can define a whole garden. You know it's wrong to think like that, but you just can't seem to stop doing it. Having to give criticism to other people is almost as bad. What if they don't like me? What if they disagree?

Worry about saying the wrong thing

Caring too much about getting it right can mean you're sometimes awkward with speech, sometimes to the point of stammering or stuttering. Or sometimes you just can't decide what to say and when to say it in a conversation, especially in a small group. So, when out with friends for a drink, or at work meetings, you perhaps just stay quiet and say very little. You may then worry about how that might affect your career, or your friendships. Is that why you don't get asked to the party, or didn't get that promotion?

Feel someone who disagrees with you must dislike you

This can be a real problem if you are involved in team meetings at work, or if you are in any kind of committee or group. It can even be upsetting if it's just a chat over coffee, or over the garden fence, about politics or the news, or where is best for a holiday. It's that inability to separate what is being talked about from whom you are talking to. It's that feeling that if they don't agree with your opinion, they don't like your opinion, and if they don't like your opinion, then they don't like you. Yet we often hear how those who argue most loudly and publicly with each other, namely politicians, at the end of a hard day can be found enjoying each other's company and having a laugh in the bar.

You think too much

Every day can seem never-ending, with so much to think about. What to say, or not to say, things you must remember, decisions to make. You can find that you can't get things people have said out of your head. Round and round they go, for hours on end, even when you go to bed. You go round in circles sometimes, trying to think it all out and make some sense of it all. But then, there you are again, right back where you started. It's all so tiring.

You feel you lack confidence and self-esteem

Worrying about what people think, and being hurt and offended, is sure to rob you of confidence and make you feel low about yourself. Your self-esteem may plummet and you may question who exactly you are. You seem to be like a leaf floating in the wind, drifting here and there according to the whims and actions of others, with no control and no direction of your own. Where are you going and why?

You often feel your nerves are on edge

This constant questioning and wondering can put your nervous system on the alert all the time, making you feel nervous, jumpy, and on edge. It is just so easy to become flustered about the smallest thing. This also causes physical tension, which can be acute and painful. You may get headaches and neck pain, which can last for days at a time. Or you can get up in the morning feeling tired and sore all over, as if you'd just run a marathon. But really it was just another day coping with your everyday life. You can feel that your brain is tired and drained from so much thinking, but still feel you can't find the answer. Why is it all so easy for everyone else?

Often feel life is frustrating

With so many decisions to contend with, life can seem difficult, and perhaps you postpone making those important decisions which could make life more interesting and fulfilling. You maybe feel that life is passing you by. You don't just go on instinct or with your gut feelings, yet feel sure you could be doing better in life. It's all impossibly frustrating.

Have problems with your mood

Ups and downs, downs and ups. That overused phrase, a 'roller-coaster ride' really does apply to you. One minute over the moon about something which has gone well. The next, sinking to the depths about something absolutely insignificant. The paper-boy being offhand with you can seem like a blatant insult. You can become tearful for almost no reason at all. Even you can't understand it, so what hope do your partner, friends and work colleagues have?

Often sleep poorly

And of course, the ultimate energy-drainer – you find that your sleep is disturbed, with vivid dreams, nightmares, and repetitive dreams. Your mind is exhausted, but it still manages to work hard while you are asleep. Even if you do get some proper sleep, you may wake frequently during the night, sometimes with a start, and then find it hard to get back to sleep again.

What now?

Did you identify with many of these descriptions? If yes, you are likely to be a sensitive person. Until today, you've probably seen that as all negative and problematic, with nothing good about it. But you can make your sensitivity work for you and not against you, and I hope this book will show you the positive side to being sensitive – yes, there is one!

First, rest assured that you are not alone. Although the world seems full of confident people, who cope with the situations you find difficult without apparent effort, there are many, many people who share your experiences in life. It's just not something people tend to talk about. People from all walks of life can find that they are sensitive for one reason or another. There are no official statistics available on the subject, as no one has so far made an effort to measure how common it is. After all it's not something people are likely to freely admit to, or talk about. It can affect all ages, men and women, and all backgrounds. But despite there being no statistics to hand, we know that it is very common. We all know someone, apart from ourselves, who is highly sensitive. And there will be ı others who are hiding it so well that you'd never suspect a thiͱ

Second, remember that being sensitive is only one part of you - you wouldn't describe a whole garden on the basis of just one plant, would you? Rest assured that you can harness your sensitivity, and use it to empower yourself so that you move forward, stronger and more in charge of your life. There are many valuable characteristics in being a sensitive person, which simply tend to be overlooked in today's frantic world. Chapter 2 starts to explore how you really can make your sensitivity work for you.

ur sensitivity work for you

irst chapter about the drawbacks of being
 ..ve, you might like to change completely, and stop being so
sensitive. This may not be the first time you've felt like that! But, not
so fast. Take time to think about this properly. You may be surprised
to hear this, but it's OK to be sensitive. You may lead a different life
from others, but being sensitive is a gift, not a character flaw. So
maybe you shouldn't change anything about yourself. Not con-
vinced?

The positive side of being highly sensitive

You may well think that there can't be a positive side to being
sensitive. This is the thing which has been making your life a misery
for as long as you can remember! This is what has been keeping you
awake at nights. What can there possibly be that is positive about it?

Here's an activity which might help you to start to change your
mind.

ACTIVITY

First, find yourself a sheet of paper, and write your name at the top.

Now, on a scale of 0 *(completely dissatisfied)*, to 100 *(completely
satisfied)*, write a number beside your name which represents how you
feel about being so sensitive.

Now on the reverse side of your paper, write your name again, and
on a scale of 0 *(having no sensitivity at all)* to 100 *(being as sensitive
as possible)*, give yourself a rating, for say, the past month.

Next, think about the people you admire most or really like – friends,
family, colleagues. Still on the same side of your sheet of paper, write
down their names underneath your own. Four or five should be
enough, but the more the better.

Now give them a score on the same sensitivity scale.

Take your time and really think about it. Be honest!

How does your score compare with the others? Higher? Lower?
About the same?

The chances are that the people you have chosen, like you, are scoring fairly high on sensitivity. Most of the people we like and admire in this world rate quite highly on the sensitivity meter. Now, why should that be? I shall explain. Here are some people I know.

Brenda L.

Brenda found life difficult. She was approaching 40, and couldn't seem to get through a week without being hurt by something said to her at her job at the local playscheme. She never felt good enough, and it was really getting to her. But Brenda always had an open door for anyone who needed a chat. Her neighbours often dropped by with their problems, and her teenage daughter could hardly make a decision without using her as a sounding board first. She was such a good listener, and always had time for people.

Paul S.

Paul, a doctor, was always being pulled up by his colleagues and the practice manager for running so late with his appointments. This really bothered him, and he went home each night stressed and upset. But what was he to do? Patients would share their problems with him, and he couldn't just ignore this, could he? In his practice, Paul was known as a really good doctor who always made time for you. You often had a bit of a wait to see him, but it was well worth it.

Su-Lin L.

Su-Lin was training to be a hairdresser. But she was sure she could do better in her relationships. She always felt she'd said or done the wrong thing, and constantly worried about simple decisions. Should she have a party, because all her friends have had one, even if she didn't really want to have one? And her friend Gail always bought her an expensive birthday present, but she couldn't afford to do that in return so what should she do? But Su-Lin has a passion for animals, and spends hours helping out as a volunteer at the local animal shelter. She is so good with them, and she often has animals which have been ill-treated home with her to give them much-needed love and attention.

Brenda, Paul and Su-Lin show us just some of the ways in which being sensitive can and does work for you. Because being sensitive comes with a whole package of other characteristics which you may have and be happy to have. And you can't have one without the other. It just doesn't work that way.

You may not have been aware of it, but you probably have some or all of the following list of positive characteristics. Don't be modest, really think about each of these. Which would you say apply to you? Be honest with yourself.

Positive characteristics

Caring
Intuitive
Very perceptive
Likeable
A good friend
Empathic
Good listener
Understanding
Enthusiastic about things
Interested in people
Sympathetic
Committed
A deep thinker
Creative
Imaginative
Intelligent
Very reliable
Trustworthy
Always have time for other people
Very good at seeing other people's point of view
Aware of subtleties
Can visualize different scenarios
Aware of consequences

Concentrate more on the positive side of being sensitive

You may often wish you could lose your sensitivity – but if you lose that, you lose everything which goes with it. Do you really want to do that? Being sensitive is a prerequisite for being a caring and intuitive person, and all the other characteristics listed above. It's all about accepting yourself for who you are, and accepting the complete package, not just bits of it.

You may have been aware of this positive side, but have discounted its importance because you tend to focus on what you see as the more negative side of being sensitive. You may feel that being sensitive is what defines you entirely as a person. But is that logical?

- Do you judge a garden by one flower in it?
- Do you choose a house by the shape of its kitchen window?
- Do you throw out all of the fruit in a bowl if one apple is mouldy?
- Do you scrap a car with a flat tyre?
- Does your impression of a whole room depend on one picture on one wall?

It all depends on how you look at the world and what you focus on. These other sides of you are probably what people like about you, and you can't have one side without the other. It's maybe why your partner loves you. These characteristics may be a source of inspiration and admiration to other people. They may be the aspects of you which you like too!

This book has not only been written to help you to cope with the problems of being sensitive, but also to show you how to recognize, value and really use the positive side of it. It will help you to channel these positive features and make the very best out of them.

Being sensitive is an important part of what makes you a unique and special individual. Because that is what you are. That's what we all are. We all pass through this world just the once. You should be all you can be, while you have this chance. There is no limit to what you can achieve if you set your mind to it. As Pablo Casals put it, 'We should say to each child: do you know what you are? You are a marvel. You are unique ... you may become a Shakespeare, a Michelangelo, a Beethoven. You have the capacity for anything.'

How you can make being sensitive work for you

First, you can be proud of all of the positive characteristics you have because, and only because, you are sensitive. Brenda, Paul and Su-Lin all came to see that they had a wonderful positive side, which they were dismissing. Brenda took a counselling course and got a new job with a local charity, and now has a spring in her step and can't wait to get to work each day. Paul took up a part-time university lecturing appointment and now enthusiastically helps to train new doctors in consultation skills. And Su-Lin found and read several books about confidence building, and realized that there were much better ways of dealing every day with other people, and now gets on as well with people as she does with animals.

Go back over the list of positive characteristics now, take a piece of paper or a notebook, and for each one, think about how you can

11

use that positive part of yourself more fully. Note how exactly you might use it in the next week, or the next month, or even further ahead. Are there longer-term opportunities in your life, which you are consistently missing out on, relating to each item on the list? You've been so busy focusing on the negative side of being sensitive, you may have missed these. Take your time, and work through the list a bit at a time over the next few days or so. Keep your notes somewhere safe.

When you are feeling down about yourself, bring out this book and read through that list of positive characteristics again. It will make you feel much better. You are most probably making this other more positive side of your sensitivity work for you already, without realizing it. You just haven't been able to see the wood for the trees. Take out the notes you've made every so often, and remind yourself of how you were planning to harness and really use your positive side. Continue to make it all work for you, and revel in being the unique and very special person you are, and in being sensitive. It's who you are.

If you feel it would help, write the list out in large writing on brightly coloured paper, and stick it up somewhere where you'll see it regularly, such as on the fridge door, or the back of the bathroom door, or on your bedroom wall. Or you can write one characteristic each on yellow stickies and leave them around where you'll see them regularly. In drawers, in books, in the car, at your bedside, wherever. Let your faint star begin to shine more and more brightly from now on, until it becomes an immense and radiant sun.

What a lack of sensitivity can do

Another way to look at this is to think of people you know who aren't highly sensitive like you. Think of people who have very little or no sensitivity at all.

You wouldn't want to be like this, would you? Perhaps some days you would, rather than feel the pain of being sensitive! But truly, you wouldn't want to have this particular cluster of characteristics. Of course, most people we meet every day will fit somewhere in between on the sensitivity scale. And we all have days when we're more sensitive than others, due to our mood, hormones, how tired we are, what happened the day before, and many other factors.

ACTIVITY

Now, think about the people you don't admire at all, or really dislike. As at the beginning of the chapter, think about friends, family, and colleagues. Write down their names on the piece of paper you were using earlier, along with the others. Four or five should be enough, but again the more the better. Now give them a score on the 0–100 sensitivity scale.

How do the scores compare with your own score, and those already on your sheet of paper?

Now think what do these people tend to have in common? Some of these characteristics perhaps?

Self-centred
Selfish
Uncaring
Aggressive
Hurtful
Dogmatic
Sometimes cruel without realizing it
Sometimes deliberately cruel
Can't put themselves in another's shoes
Don't think things through
Inattentive
Rude
Manipulative

Spend too much time focusing on being too sensitive?

'I cannot give you the formula for success, but I can give you the formula for failure – which is: try to please everybody.' Wise words from American newspaper editor Herbert Swope, and ones that sensitive people could perhaps sometimes pay more attention to!

Do you spend a lot of your time reacting to life in the way described in Chapter 1? Do you spend even more time being annoyed that you react in these ways, and wondering how you can change, and be less sensitive? Much of your precious time and energy is spent focusing on this. In today's high-speed world, time is too precious to spend in this way.

But what can you do? You've tried so hard, and tried everything you can think of, to stop being sensitive. You've put up with people's jibes and criticisms. Too soft. Too touchy. Stop being so soft. And when you were younger, 'don't be such a cry-baby'.

If you act proudly and confidently, sure of yourself and pleased to be who you are, and stop apologizing for yourself all the time, people will react to you differently, and stop making critical jibes and comments about your behaviour. How often do you use the word 'sorry' each day?

But why me?

It's time to pause for breath and step back a bit from things now. You are probably wondering why you are a sensitive person in the first place. This is a question I'm sure you've asked yourself over and over again. You've probably got your own various theories about this. And yes, there are many possible reasons. But, no, none is your fault. In the next chapter we'll think about some of these. See if you can identify with anything.

3

Why you are too sensitive

Just knowing why you are sensitive won't change a thing. If you have a broken leg, knowing that you slipped on some ice won't mend the fracture. But it does help you to understand and accept what has happened. And in understanding and in acceptance, there is peace, satisfaction, and a feeling of being more in control of your life. These are things the over-sensitive person doesn't often feel.

Working out why you are sensitive

Working out the reasons for being sensitive is useful because it helps you to:

- see that maybe it wasn't your fault;
- see that maybe it was someone else's fault;
- feel more in control of your life;
- stop blaming yourself for seeming weak;
- see that it was just bad luck or circumstances;
- understand your life better;
- see that the current state of affairs doesn't need to continue;
- believe that you can change;
- see what you might do to help make your sensitivity work for you, not against you.

We are going to look at a list of possible reasons why people can become sensitive. Just one of these is enough to turn an outgoing and confident person into a sensitive one, but the more of them which have been active in your life, the more sensitive you can become. And of course it's a vicious circle because once you are a bit sensitive, it is so much easier to become a little more, and a little more.

I am not in the business of apportioning blame here. The kind of upbringing you had, or the school you attended, may have played a part, but we don't know the reasons for these circumstances being exactly as they were. We don't know the full picture, and people often do what turns out to be wrong for us, with the best of motives. What we are seeking here are reasons to help us understand; we're not looking for people to blame.

In this chapter I'll explain some of the many reasons why people can become sensitive. Think about your own background as you read. Don't worry if some of the ideas make you feel a bit emotional, or if they make you remember and relive past experiences. Letting that emotion come to the surface, and releasing it, can only do you good. Most people find this, and the emotion soon subsides. Pent-up feelings of frustration, anger and resentment are better out than in. But for a few people, the emotion aroused can be stronger and more long-lasting, and if this happens to you, talking to your doctor or a qualified counsellor can help.

I first met Joan very recently. She had just retired, and had completely lost her direction in her life.

Joan C.

Joan grew up in the 1950s when parents tended to be very strict, and 'children should be seen and not heard.' Criticism was seen to be good for children, and praise was only going to encourage a swollen head. Very different from today. But Joan was a creative and imaginative child who always had something to say, and enjoyed dancing and singing. She was constantly being scolded, and told to be quiet, both at home and at school. All she ever seemed to hear about her dancing and singing and her imaginative ideas was criticism. Over the years of her childhood, Joan gradually grew quieter and more careful in what she said and did so that she could avoid harsh words from teachers and her parents. She grew more introverted, and eager to please. Joan was now 61 and had just retired from her work as an office administrator. She had split up with her husband Jack many years ago, as they were constantly bickering, and he said he couldn't cope with her moods any more. All her adult life she had been the sensitive type, eager to please everyone and not make a fuss and draw attention to herself. But she now felt life had passed her by, and she'd missed out on so many important things.

Joan's upbringing and schooling had played a crucial role in her becoming a sensitive adult, whose life just hadn't lived up to her expectations. But she was ready to change all that.

Reasons why people may be sensitive

Below is a list of some of the reasons for a person being sensitive. But remember, if you are sensitive you also have all those positive features which we talked about in Chapter 2, so it's not all bad news. We're just looking for you to understand it all a bit better, to help you to move on. Did any of these leave their mark on you? Underline any which did.

Your carer or parent/s

Very sensitive themselves
Disliked over-confidence in their children
Criticized other people a lot
Criticized each other a lot
Argued often
Prone to moodiness

How you were 'parented' or cared for as a child

Unfair or harsh discipline or punishment of any kind
Corporal punishment
Lots of criticism, but no praise or little praise
No logic or predictability to praise or criticism

Your carer or parent's relationship with you

Resented you for some reason (e.g. 'If it wasn't for you . . .')
Being told you weren't good enough
Not being loved
Not seeming to be loved
Being loved only if you were 'good'
Being put-down all the time
Abuse of any kind
Comparing you unfavourably with others
Always being blamed for things going wrong
Favouring another brother or sister over you
Little or no attention
Lots of unhelpful criticism of mistakes or failures
Lots of unhelpful criticism for lack of knowledge
Not allowed to have your own point of view
Not being listened to
Not being taken seriously

General home situation when growing up

Very sheltered with little experience outside the home
Few visitors at home
Your friends not allowed to visit
Having visitors was a big event
Forced into the limelight
Forced to compete with others
Spent time in care

Lots of upheaval
Under-privileged
Over-privileged
Discriminated against

Brothers and sisters

Unsupportive
Competitive
Bullying (verbal, emotional, or physical)
Being a middle child
Being the oldest child
Being the youngest child
Being an only child

School days

Bullying (physical, verbal, or emotional)
Frightening teacher
Violent teacher
Critical teacher
Picked on by teacher or pupils
Unfair or harsh discipline or punishment (any kind)
Corporal punishment, especially if unfair
Few friends due to constant moves or isolation
Manipulative friends
Discriminated against

Distressing or traumatic experiences growing up

Loss of someone or something important to you, through no fault
of your own
Serious accident
Living in a non-peaceful environment
Parents splitting up distressed you
Parental behaviour distressed you
Domestic violence
Situations or experiences which have left you feeling guilty
High anxiety producing unpleasant symptoms
Discriminated against
Being in care, with poor support

Current life experiences

Being bullied at work or at home
Domestic abuse (physical or mental)
Critical, moody circle of friends

Critical, moody partner
Critical work colleagues
Moody work colleagues

Now look back at those you've underlined and think about these questions:

1 Are there only a few underlined, or many?
2 Does anything surprise you?
3 Are they spread evenly throughout the list, or concentrated under certain headings?
4 What might this all mean for you?
5 In what ways does knowing why you are so sensitive help you?

But there's one more area which causes sensitivity which we haven't covered yet. Have you spotted it? Yes, we haven't looked at *you* yourself, and any role you may have in being highly sensitive. Don't worry, I'm not going to blame you for anything.

What makes you sensitive?

What about your own make-up as a person?

Elizabeth B.
Elizabeth had just started working in an estate agent's. She had recently divorced from Joe after 15 difficult years of marriage. The marriage was fine for the first few years, but she couldn't cope with Joe being so unemotional and unsupportive. Elizabeth always seemed to be worrying about something that happened at work that day, and wanted to talk it through and sort it out in her head. But Joe always had his head in a paper or watching TV, and didn't react much to what she was saying. Elizabeth couldn't cope with the hurt and offence this caused. But now she was finding her new job difficult, because she felt that her work colleagues were reacting in the same way. She couldn't understand it, and spoke to her parents about it. They said they had had problems when they were younger too, as her mother often found her father didn't give her enough support when she was worrying about something someone had said, or a problem with a friend.

One of the main reasons for being sensitive is that you've simply inherited it from your parents. Was one or both of them like you? These things can skip around the generations, so have a think about your extended family. Was there anyone who behaved similarly to you? This can actually be an intrinsic part of your nervous system, no different from whether you are short or tall, or have green or blue eyes. Your nervous system may be a very reactive one, prone to react more strongly and more quickly to life's difficulties and experiences than everyone else's. You've heard of the expression 'highly strung', and this may apply to you. Everyone's nervous system reacts to stimulation from outside the body, some more than others. You may have a more than usually sensitive nervous system, often inherited, which makes you more prone to nervous arousal and perhaps nervous overload. In later chapters, we will help you with this. You may also find a book I have written with a medical colleague, Dr Ken Hambly, helpful too – *Coping with a Stressed Nervous System* (published by Sheldon Press in 2005).

Another reason you may be sensitive is that somewhere along the line, you've gained a habit of tending to focus more on your own viewpoint and role in a situation, and ignoring or underestimating the role of other people. Take Sanjay for example.

Sanjay P.
Sanjay was a teacher in a large school, and for the past few weeks, he had found that the staffroom went quiet whenever he came in. He was convinced that they were all talking about him, and that no one liked him any more. What could he have done, he wondered desperately. He worried at home, and talked about it incessantly to his wife. But, what he didn't know was that the staff had other reasons for going quiet when he came into the room. In fact, he always came in with another colleague from his department, who was having an affair with the deputy head, which was what they had been talking about when Sanjay came in. It was nothing to do with him.

It's easy to feel that we are the cause of everything which happens to us and around us. But it isn't often like that at all. All of life's experiences and situations are the sum of a multitude of parts and people. Chapter 11 should be able to help you with this.

Finally, we are all born with some fairly basic character traits, thanks to our genes, our physiology and our brain chemistry. These may adapt and change through our experiences of life, but there are some strong aspects and strands of our personality and behaviour which still remain, no matter what. As we've said already, you may have directly inherited a tendency to be sensitive. But you may have other character traits which have led in a more indirect way to your becoming sensitive.

Being too much of a perfectionist is a typical example. For many people this is not a problem. For others, being a perfectionist can mean that your standards are such that you may be easily hurt and offended by others especially with your need for perfection in your relationships. This can impinge on your life at work, at home and socially with friends.

Similarly, if you are more of an introvert than an extravert this means you may well become more sensitive in your dealings with others, perhaps because you have simply had less practice socially. Not enjoying being the centre of attention is another personality trait which usually means you will be sensitive, almost by definition, as this arises from caring too much about what others think about you.

Moving on

I hope that this chapter has been revealing and interesting for you. Simply being aware of the kinds of experiences, physiology and personality traits which may have led to your being sensitive may provide quite a powerful release for you. Just having this kind of understanding can ease the guilt and the endless questioning, 'Why me?'. It takes the mystery out of it, and gives you back control of your own life.

As sure as night follows day, being too sensitive, if not understood properly, brings in its wake poor self-image, lack of confidence, anxiety, tension, being moody or having mood swings, lack of assertiveness, and a feeling of a lack of control of your life. The remainder of the book will show you lots and lots of ways to cope better with these and other negative effects of being too sensitive, so that you can make the positive aspects work better for you, without your being dragged down by those which are more negative.

4

How to be more confident – on your terms

When I talk to people who are highly sensitive, the idea of not having enough confidence comes up again and again. We've already talked about this in Chapter 1. And yet, having confidence is so important to us all in our everyday lives, and is something which other people seem to take for granted. It seems to come so easily to everybody else, and yet you find it so very difficult.

It probably comes as no surprise to you that people who lack confidence often have a very negative self-image, or in other words, low self-esteem. It kind of goes with the territory, as we saw in Chapter 1. You are likely to find yourself feeling shy, reserved, and generally dissatisfied with your life. You may even dislike yourself, and blame yourself for all your problems. How you see yourself is at the heart of the matter when it comes to problems with confidence. This is where we should begin.

How do you see yourself?

This negative self-image of yourself is of course completely mistaken. As we've seen already, it is a perception of yourself, which you have developed as a result of your experiences, and bears no relation at all to the reality. It's as if you are perpetually looking at yourself through one of those distorting mirrors which they used to have at the funfair. What you need to do is to stop looking at a distorted image, and see yourself in a true mirror.

Sometimes, instead of having a negative self-image, someone with low confidence can simply have an unclear picture of who and what they really are. Again, experiences in childhood can produce this unsettling effect. It's as if you are looking at yourself, not in a distorting mirror this time, but in a mirror in a poorly lit room, and are finding it hard to see yourself at all.

Let's try a simple activity which can be very revealing about how you currently see yourself, and which is good for suggesting areas you might like to start to work on if you want to move towards a truer reflection of yourself.

ACTIVITY

Without thinking too deeply about it, try writing 20 short statements about yourself, answering the question 'Who am I?', and beginning with the words, 'I am . . .'.

Just write whatever comes into your head.

Give yourself no more than ten minutes to do this:

I am _____

I am _____

I am _____

I am _____

I am _____

I am _____

I am _____

I am _____

I am _____

I am _____

I am _____

I am _____

I am _____

I am _____

I am _____

I am _____

I am _____

I am _____

I am _____

I am _____

Now, look back over what you've written. What you will have produced is a kind of thumbnail sketch of how you see yourself and your roles in life. Here are some questions to think about.

Did you find it difficult or even impossible to generate 20 answers to the question, 'Who am I?'. This is not uncommon, especially if you have low confidence in yourself. But it may also suggest that your life is somewhat limited, and that you should consider broadening your horizons. It also suggests that you may have a picture of yourself and your identity, which is not too clear. You may not be sure of who you really are.

Perhaps you found it easy to fill in the 20 statements, and could have gone on to produce some more. This might suggest that you are spreading yourself a little too thinly, and are trying to do too much, and be too much to too many people. Or maybe you're skipping from interest to interest, and relationship to relationship, becoming bored quickly because nothing satisfies you for long. This is a common reaction to low self-esteem and lack of identity. But it can make it difficult for you to focus on who you really are, and to feel secure and confident. Perhaps you need to cut back a bit on things, and sort out and concentrate on a few meaningful priorities. Or maybe you just need to become more organized in what you do.

Now have a look again at the top two or three statements. These usually give a picture of your core identity. People tend to write down the most important parts of how they see themselves first. Are you happy with this picture? Or are you painting a picture which is dissatisfying? Could this have anything to do with your lack of confidence? Now look at the statements further down your list, if you have written more. Would you like some of these to have come much further up your list, indicating a higher importance? Think about how you might go about making these changes.

Do a lot of your answers to the question 'Who am I?' depend on your role in relation to other people? For example, did you give many answers along the lines of 'I am a mother', 'I am a son', 'I am a good neighbour', and very few along the lines of ' I am Caroline', 'I am an artist', 'I am kind' or 'I am good at sport'. In other words, does who you are depend too much on other people and how you relate to them? This can give you a somewhat shadowy and tenuous sense of identity, subject to the views and whims of others, and make it hard to have confidence in yourself. Sometimes people find themselves asking 'Where am *I*?' after working on this activity. Let's try to answer that question for you.

Thinking about your achievements

After that bit of soul-searching, let's focus on something very positive and very down to earth as we begin to build up your self-image and sense of identity.

Sometimes when we lack confidence we can lose sight of the fact that we have achieved much in our lives. Typically, those who lack confidence tend to forget about these achievements. The achievements of others are down to their being clever or hard-working, but your own are just down to luck or someone else being kind to you. Or you may feel that it is big-headed to be pleased with something you've done. Or perhaps you may feel that your achievements are worthless because they don't meet someone else's criteria (i.e. you are a successful teacher whereas your parents always wanted you to be a doctor). Wrong. Your achievements are your achievements, and are down to you. They are for you to be proud and satisfied about.

Listing your achievements

As you can see, it isn't just a matter of discounting your own achievements while valuing those of others. It's also a question of not even recognizing an achievement when you see it! I hope the activity on page 26 will help you to see your achievements in a more positive light. Try this now.

Hopefully you now see your achievements in a different light. If you found that you had very few ticks in the list, maybe you should think about finding time to try out some of the items listed, or something else you've always wanted to do. It's never too late. 'To be what we are, and to become what we are capable of becoming, is the only end in life,' as Robert Louis Stevenson said.

Your skills, strengths and talents

People who lack confidence often feel that they have few skills. Or, if they do have skills, they feel that everyone else does these things better than they do. But there are many, many skills, not just the obvious ones like painting, playing a musical instrument or running fast, or work-based skills like giving presentations, writing reports or installing a central heating system. In fact, as Thomas Edison said, if we did everything we were capable of, we would astound ourselves!

This section will show you that there are lots and lots of skills which we all use every day, but which we just don't notice, or which we take for granted. It can be helpful when trying to improve your confidence if you can become more aware of these skills, which you undoubtedly have.

ACTIVITY

Go through the achievements listed below, and tick those which apply to you:

- ☐ Being a good friend to someone
- ☐ Learning a new hobby or pastime
- ☐ Bringing up a child or children
- ☐ Being an active member of a club or group (any kind)
- ☐ Working on a community project (any kind)
- ☐ A job or work you've done
- ☐ Travel within UK
- ☐ Travel abroad
- ☐ Learning to drive
- ☐ Learning to swim
- ☐ Completing a course (any kind)
- ☐ Learning and participating in a sport
- ☐ Learning to use a computer
- ☐ Looking after a pet
- ☐ Learning another language
- ☐ Giving regularly to a charity (any kind)
- ☐ Writing a story, poem, article or book (any kind)
- ☐ Learning to play a musical instrument
- ☐ Learning to dance
- ☐ Learning a practical skill in the home (cooking, decorating, etc.)
- ☐ Keeping plants or having a garden

Anything else we've missed?

Go back over your list and put a (1) next to what you feel is your main achievement, then a (2) for your next best achievement, and so on until you've numbered at least three or four.

ACTIVITY

Here is a long list of skills, talents, and strengths! Take your time, and work your way through it, marking each item on the list with the number which best fits how you would currently rate yourself, on a scale of 0 (*doesn't apply to you, or not at all good at it*) to 5 (*I'm very good at this*). Remember, *honesty essential, but no modesty allowed.* Don't soul-search too much on the answers, just rate each according to how you are in general, most days, on each item.

Skills, talents and strengths	Rating
Personal:	
Determined	＿＿
Honest	＿＿
Patient	＿＿
Have a sense of humour	＿＿
Caring	＿＿
Considerate	＿＿
Natural warmth	＿＿
Confident	＿＿
Sensible	＿＿
Positive	＿＿
Trustworthy	＿＿
Hard-working	＿＿
Practical:	
Mending things	＿＿
Being able to work steadily	＿＿
Working with computers	＿＿
Working with machinery/gadgets	＿＿
Cooking	＿＿
DIY	＿＿
Understanding how things work	＿＿
Working with animals	＿＿
Working with plants	＿＿
Social:	
Friendly	＿＿
Being sensitive to other people's moods	＿＿
Being tactful	＿＿
Good with children	＿＿
Diplomatic	＿＿

Getting on with other people _____
Expressing feelings _____
Helping others _____
Listening to others _____
Being reliable _____

Thinking and learning:
Learning new things _____
Remembering things _____
Thinking quickly and clearly _____
Having ideas _____
Being imaginative _____
Being inventive _____
Analysing things _____
Solving problems _____
Curious about new ideas _____

Practical communication:
Explaining things clearly in writing _____
Letter-writing _____
Report-writing _____
Making a presentation _____
Explaining things clearly by voice _____
Being interesting when speaking _____
Being persuasive when speaking _____
Using email _____

Leadership:
Taking the lead when needed _____
Staying calm in a crisis _____
Taking the initiative _____
Taking risks (not physical) _____
Organizing people _____

Practical organization:
Able to be efficient _____
Attention to detail _____
Collecting and sorting facts and information _____
Being logical _____
Researching a subject _____
Managing money _____
Creating a plan _____

Following a pattern or plan   ____
Working with figures   ____
Organizing time   ____
Coordinating lots of things   ____
Completing tasks on time   ____

Artistic/Creative:
Writing stories or poems   ____
Writing articles or scripts   ____
Music   ____
Dance   ____
Painting   ____
Drama   ____
Pottery   ____
Designing things   ____
Gardening   ____

Physical:
Keeping fit   ____
Keeping strong   ____
Staying calm under pressure   ____
Looking good   ____
Having lots of energy   ____
A sport or other activity   ____

What are your main skills/talents/strengths? Yes, you do have many you probably hadn't thought of, or hadn't counted for some reason. How many did you score over 0? Now go back over the list, and put an asterisk (*) next to your seven or eight highest scoring items. Now look the whole list over again. Are your asterisks mostly under just one or two of the headings? If so, which one/s, and what might this tell you about yourself? Has this activity helped to build a more positive and clear self-image for you?

What is important to me?

It's time to consider the bigger issues in life, and how important these are to you. This is another broad strand of your identity, and one which can really underline who you are.

ACTIVITY

Work your way through this list, and as before, mark each item with the number which best fits how you would currently rate how important that item is to you on a score of 0 (*doesn't matter to me at all*) to 5 (*extremely important to me*).

As before, don't soul-search too much on the answers; your first thought is probably the most accurate. Rate each according to how important you feel each item is to you, in general, most of the time.

Subject area	Explanation: It's important to me to . . .	Rating
Helping others	Help others in need	____
Independence	Be able to work or act in the way I want, without others telling me what to do	____
Learning	Have the chance to learn or study new things	____
Variety	Have lots of different things to do	____
Novelty	Move on to new things regularly	____
Work	Have the right kind of work for me	____
Challenge	Feel stretched and stimulated by new ideas and/ or activities	____
Approval	Feel appreciated, valued and needed	____
Leadership	Be able to organize and be responsible for other people	____

Happiness	Enjoy life and be happy and contented	____
Views and ideals	Have strong ideals and principles	____
Surroundings	Live or work in the right surroundings for me	____
Security	Feel secure at home or work	____
Affection	Enjoy the company of family and friends	____
Money	Make a lot of money	____
Status	Be well known and/or respected by others and/or have high status	____
Physical fitness	Be very fit	____

Go back over this list, and put an asterisk (*) next to your five highest scoring items. Do these five surprise you at all? Did you realize these were important to you? Does your life currently allow you to meet all of these needs? If not, think about how you might go about meeting these needs. Give it some real thought. This will help you to gain a much better sense of who you are to build on.

Finding yourself

Complete the following short questionnaire honestly, adding to it anything you like. You could also take out some photos of yourself as a child, growing up, and as an adult, and right up to today. Think of at least one (and more if you can) positive thing you can say about yourself at the time of your life when each photograph was taken. Then over the next few weeks and months, read this questionnaire over regularly, to refresh and reinforce the ideas in your mind.

PERSONAL QUESTIONNAIRE

My name is _____

I am a woman/man, my age is _____ next birthday, which is on

_____

I was born in _____ and weighed _____

My mother's name is/was _____ and my father's name is/was

_____

I was given my first name because _____

_____ and I like/dislike it.

I grew up mainly in _____

At school, my main achievements were _____

_____

_____

My best memory of my school days is _____

My favourite meal when I was growing up was _____

And my favourite snack was _____

The pet I got most pleasure from was _____

My favourite pastime was _____

My best holiday memory as a child is _____

My favourite meal as a grown-up is _____

My favourite pastime/s as a grown-up are _____

_____

_____

I really enjoy these pastimes because _____

_____

My favourite people in my life are _____

_____

_____

I like them because _____

_____

_____

The people listed here really like me _____

_____

_____

They like me because _____

_____

_____

I am really good at these things _____

_____

_____

I wish I could be better at these things _____

_____

_____

I really like these things about my life _____

_____

_____

I don't really like these things about my life _____

_____

_____

In my life it is important that I _____

In my life it is important to me that other people _____

My job is _____

I chose it because _____

_____

I like these things about my job _____

_____

_____

I don't like these things about my job _____

_____

_____

I like these things about the world _____

_____

I'd like to see these things made better in the world _____

_____

My favourite colour is _____

My favourite flower is _____

My favourite time of year is _____

My best achievements in life so far have been _____

_____

_____

My pet hates about people are _____

My favourite TV programmes are _____

My favourite place in the world is _____

I adore the smell of _____

If I had to choose four words to describe who I really am, they would be

_____

In my lifetime, it's important to me that I _____

_____

_____

_____

_____

Your social skills

Now that you have a much better idea of who you are, you can start from today and grow, nurture and develop your identity. Many people find they knew who they were all along. They just needed time to think about it, and see it in writing to 'give them permission' to be that person.

With your new-found identity, let's think about how you can behave with more confidence. Most people find certain social situations awkward and anxiety-making. If you are sensitive, social situations can pose all kinds of problems. Always wondering what kind of impression you're making, and whether you are saying the right thing.

This section will provide ideas for making these situations a little easier. As with most suggestions in this book, steps towards change can take time and not a little effort, but the rewards will make it all worthwhile. All new relationships – from friends and partners, to work colleagues, to new neighbours – begin with social skills. We're not born with these skills, we need to learn them – and we can always be improving them, too.

In Chapter 7, we will look at how difficult it can be to say 'no' to people, and we'll suggest ways of doing this more effectively. But if you have problems with socializing, saying 'no' to an invitation can be the easiest thing in the world. Armed with a wealth of genuine and not so genuine reasons, saying 'no' couldn't be easier! In this area, try not to let the word 'no' be so much on the tip of your tongue. When invited to attend a social event, or go somewhere with friends, pause, take a deep breath and say 'yes'.

Social skills are like riding a bike. They do not come naturally. They are learned mainly in childhood and early adulthood from our parents, our family, teachers, our peers and from others. We learn them without realizing it, and mainly by imitating others. There are many reasons why this process may have worked inefficiently for you. Parents with poor social skills themselves, low levels of social interaction, and excessive criticism, can all put you at a disadvantage.

But it's never too late to learn these skills, or improve on them. You just have to take things slowly, one step at a time, and be prepared for a few setbacks. Let's begin with one of the key parts of socializing: making conversation. I focus on conversation between two people, but everything said applies just as much to small groups of people.

Conversation and listening skills

Key to improving your conversation skills is not to learn to be a better talker, but to become a better listener. Problems with this arise because you are too concerned about what you are saying, and concentrating too much on the impression you are making. This gives you no time actually to listen to what the other person is saying. But it all becomes much easier if you can simply relax, forget yourself, and become genuinely interested in the other person. Other people can be really interesting, if you just listen to them! Remember, listening is not a passive process, as you might think, but an active one. Here are some suggestions.

- Let the other person share the talking and listening roughly equally – in other words, take turns.

- Relax, so that you can focus better on what's being said.
- Focus on the other person, not yourself.
- Really listen and pay attention.
- Actively engage with what is being said.
- Allow yourself to become genuinely interested in what's being said.
- Notice their body language.
- Hear the emotion in the person's words and in their voice.
- Get behind the words to what the person is thinking and feeling and why.
- Use facial expression and body language to show that you've understood, or are surprised, or amused or whatever.

Talking

What about the talking part of a conversation? As already said, if you can listen actively, you will find it much easier when it's your turn. Here are some other thoughts which may be useful. Remember, though, to take this one step at a time, and not to try to do too much at once. Otherwise you risk becoming very tongue-tied indeed!

Inevitably on social occasions, we are required to engage in 'small talk'. This can sometimes be a problem. For people you already know, small talk at a social event usually begins with simple 'How are you?' sorts of questions, moving on to asking how their partner or family are. These sorts of questions will usually be reciprocated and asked of you, so come prepared with some basic information ready to give in reply. Just the basics, no need to go into great detail.

For people you've never met, conversation is more likely to begin with introductions, then move to comments about the event you're attending and how you got there, then to simple general discussion of where you're from, whether you work and if so at what, and so on. People like to get a thumbnail sketch of someone before moving forward with small talk. No point in asking someone who's been unemployed for three years where they went on holiday that summer. The more practice you get at small talk, the better you'll be at it.

Sometimes, the reason small talk is difficult, especially after the early stage we've just described, is because you actually don't have much to say. This is not meant to be cruel! It's just that typical small-talk topics are not always of interest to everyone. You might be the kind of person who doesn't pay much attention to the stuff of small talk – what's in the news, community events, holidays, popular TV programmes, fashion trends, sport and so on. If you are from a younger or older age group, the topics discussed may be a bit different, but the advice is still the same.

It helps if you can keep an eye on the news and current affairs, even if you don't usually. Buy a popular newspaper or magazine regularly to keep up with what's in and what's not. Watch a few of the most popular TV programmes for your age group, just to keep in touch. It's all worth the effort. Having a few thoughts and ideas ready on a range of everyday and non-controversial topics will never go wrong. However, it's always best to steer clear of potentially controversial subjects, at least until you build up your confidence!

You may find small talk boring, many people do; but unfortunately, this is what socializing is often about, and it's how almost all meaningful relationships begin.

It is important that you be yourself, and don't try to put on an act of any kind. All we're trying to do here is brush up on your skills, not make you into somebody else. Anyway, being a little shy can be quite attractive and bring out the protective instinct in others.

Common topics to open a conversation, and continue small talk on are:

- a recent news story
- how you got to the 'event' you're attending
- the 'host' of the event
- the purpose of the event
- the food or hospitality
- what the person does for a living, or retired?/unemployed?
- where you're from
- whether you've been here before
- the weather
- how the person is
- comments on how the 'event' is going

Reflecting back to the other person what they've just told you is a very powerful way to show you are listening with interest. It is also likely to encourage someone to go on and tell you more. If someone has just related to you all about their car problems over the past week, you might say, 'You've had it really bad this past week. You must be feeling annoyed about that.' They may well respond, 'You bet I do. It never seems to end. Just when I thought it was fixed. With my last car, it was all very different, I . . .'

If someone relates to you an experience in which they have shown a strength of some kind, it is very helpful to give them feedback

ACTIVITY

Try making up a list of open questions that you might use in the kinds of conversation you are likely to be involved in. Open questions are those which you can't answer with a simple, one- or two-word answer: How is your mother? What did you think of the concert? How was your journey here? What made you come to the gym? Closed questions can be answered with one or two words: Where do you live? How many children do you have? When does this finish? They can stop small talk before it's even begun, and feel like an interrogation if you're at the receiving end of it! Get a sheet of paper or a notepad, and try to make up at least one question to start a conversation just now, and one or two to follow up with. (You can add to this list over the next few weeks or months if you want to.)

---

about that strength. 'You were very brave doing that.' 'You showed such kindness there.' This can be very effective and help to build a relationship with that person.

When it's your turn to talk

Here's a summary, along with a few more ideas.

Don't hog the floor – share it equally.
Be consistent.
Be genuine.
Respect and like the other person.
Wait for a natural pause before you speak.
Try not to interrupt the speaker.
Use person's name when appropriate.
React to what the person is saying.
Have an open mind.
Ask an open question.
Reflect back what's been said.
Ask for more information.
Give feedback on what's been said.
Sum up what's been said so far.
You can also contribute to the conversation at appropriate moments by nodding, or saying 'uh-huh' or 'mm-hmm'.

Your rights

One of the reasons we can act in a submissive or overly sensitive way in our dealings with others is because we feel people's needs are more important than ours. One aspect of respecting yourself and knowing your own needs is tied up with your rights as a person. We can lack confidence simply because we don't realize that it's not just other people who have rights, but that we do too.

We're not talking about legal rights here, but the everyday rights we should all have as human beings. Organizations such as Amnesty

---

ACTIVITY

Read through the list of rights slowly, and <u>underline</u> any which you have trouble with giving to yourself:

I have the right:
To express myself.
To express myself in my own way.
To express myself in my own time.
To my own point of view.
To have my own values.
To be treated as an equal.
To ask others to listen to me.
To make a mistake.
To say 'no'.
To say what I want.
To fail if I try.
To try again.
To be a leader.
To express my feelings.
To be treated with respect.
To make my own decisions.
To choose for myself.
To change my mind.
To decide for myself what is best for me.
To ask for what I want.
To be angry sometimes.
To take control of a situation.
To start again.

International campaign every day for people whose human rights have been denied them by dogmatic and extreme regimes. But often people who lack confidence are denying themselves some of their basic human rights every day, without any pressure being brought to bear, or even being aware that they are doing it. Why? Because their upbringing or life experiences have led them to believe very deeply that they don't have these rights.

So what rights are we talking about? Well, here is a new 'Bill of Rights' for you.

Take another look at what you've underlined. For each item, think about why you have a problem with it. Have you been denied that right so often or so strongly (or both) in the past that you came to believe that you simply didn't have that right, or that you didn't deserve that right? Well, it's not true. You are a worthwhile human being. There will be never be another person just like you. You have these rights, and deserve these rights like everyone else. Nobody else's rights are more important than yours.

When there is a clash of people's rights, the assertive thing to do is compromise, not suppress *your* rights in favour of the other person's. But how often has that happened in the world? How often has it happened in your world? More on the subject of assertiveness in Chapter 7.

Body language

It has been estimated that people we meet for the first time form around 90 per cent of their impression of us within the first 90 seconds of meeting or seeing us. How much are you likely to say in the first 90 seconds? Probably very little, usually simple introductions and everyday comments. Not much to form an opinion of someone. But even what you say in these first few seconds is likely to be overlooked in favour of the impression you make with how you sound, what your handshake was like, and what you are wearing. Think about your own interactions with other people. Watch out for this when you next meet someone, or when you are introduced to a new person at work, or when you are standing in the supermarket queue. Notice how you form impressions of people very quickly, without really being aware of it. It's something we all do. It helps us to make sense of our world.

But we also all know that first impressions can be terribly wrong. Everyone has had experience of this. This may be happening to you.

Even if you feel that you are saying all the right things, your body language might be letting you down. Because our body language can be saying something quite different from what we are saying verbally – and the body language is usually the overriding and most accurate one, which people believe if there is a choice. We all interpret body language without thinking. We are usually completely unaware of how other people's body language is affecting us. We are just aware of the conclusions we draw from it.

If your lack of confidence is showing through your body language, it's worth doing something about it. This may be showing itself clearly whenever you meet someone or enter a room, giving people a negative image of you, and getting you off to a bad start. It's then a bit of a vicious circle, with how people react to you making you feel even less confident, which shows in your body language, and so on.

But we can easily do something about that. This section will give you lots of ideas. The beginning of this chapter should also help because if you improve your feeling of self-worth and increase your understanding of who you are, this will automatically show in your body language.

This is how good actors can become such different people so easily. First they get the posture and body language just right. For example, David Jason is equally believable as Del Boy in *Only Fools and Horses* and Detective Inspector Frost in *A Touch of Frost*. Michael Crawford completely transformed himself from a whimpering Frank Spencer into the powerful depiction of an imposing Phantom of the Opera. Actors like Patricia Routledge, Tom Courtney and Robert de Niro seem to be able to transform themselves simply by use of posture and voice, so that we are sometimes surprised when we see the 'real' them for the first time, in a chat show for example.

There is a lot in how you walk, stand and come into a room, which lets people know how confident you are. But you can be like an actor too, and can practise having the body language of a confident person. Practise this at home when no one's about, until it becomes natural to you, and you won't need to think about it. The best of it is that if you stand and walk confidently, you will actually feel and be more confident. Try it and see!

Don't try to do too much

If you try to remember all of these ideas about body language all at once, you'll come into a room looking very strange, and maybe slightly confused! Not a good idea! It's best to concentrate on one thing at a time, maybe your general posture, and work on that for a while, before moving on maybe to what you're doing with your hands, your head, or your eyes. There's plenty of time. Body language is the habit of a lifetime. It takes a little time and effort to make changes. But the positive side of this is that with each change, the next one comes a little more easily, and the feedback of improvements in how other people react to these changes is also likely to encourage you and improve your confidence in what you're doing.

The remainder of this section on body language will give you some more ideas on how to make your body behave more confidently. Read through and see if some of these will be useful for you. You could underline anything you find particularly useful so that it's easy to find if you're reading back over this chapter later on.

General suggestions for confident body language

Much of the body language which shows a lack of confidence arises from a need for comfort. We are nervous and ill at ease, and unsure of ourselves, and just like children, seek comfort from contact with another person or object. Just as a child runs to his or her mother, or clings to a security blanket or doll, we may, as adults, cling to a handbag or a even a pen, or make sure we have someone beside us at social events. Stooped posture and poor eye contact also arise from a wish to make ourselves as small and unnoticeable as we can. Tension due to anxiety can make us hunch up our shoulders, towards our ears. People may even ask you if you are feeling cold because of this. So let those shoulders drop, and let them relax. More on how to relax in Chapters 6 and 7.

An open and relaxed posture is usually best, preferably with little or nothing in your hands. Open posture means comfortably upright, shoulders comfortably back, head up, with no barriers formed by your hands or arms. Arms comfortably by your side, or open hands resting easily on your lap when sitting, convey quiet, relaxed confidence. The relaxation and breathing exercises later in this book will make this posture easier to achieve, so remember to practise these.

Lack of confidence can make you form a fist with your hands, or cling to a handbag, briefcase or drink. This will be noticed unconsciously, or even consciously by those you are with. Avoid folding your arms, as this creates a barrier, and can be interpreted as a lack of interest, or even disagreement or disapproval which may inhibit other people from talking to you. When standing, avoid leaning on furniture or the doorway. Again, this can be done for comfort, but can come over as somewhat odd, or even intimidating or dominating.

When sitting, sit up well. This is good for your back too! Slouching into a chair or a corner can be comforting, but looks defensive and uninviting. So sit up and lean forward a little towards others you might be talking to. This shows interest and encourages people. Crossed legs or ankles also tend to appear defensive or negative.

Practise standing or sitting in this relaxed way when you're on your own. You can do this at the same time as practising those relaxation and breathing techniques later in the book. It can be difficult at first if you've been used to holding on to something for comfort. But it will come. It's time to let go.

Handshakes

Shaking hands on meeting someone can give the other person an important – and lasting – first impression of us. We all know how unappealing the 'dead-fish' or 'cold-fish' handshake is – cold and limp, and not engaging with the other person's hand at all. The best form of handshake is single-handed, dry, and fairly firm, with both your hand and that of the person you are meeting in a vertical position. This, teamed with good eye contact and a warm smile, is an assertive and confident form of greeting. It will get you off to a great start. Avoid giving a palm down handshake as this indicates dominance, or palm upward as this suggests that you are passive or submissive.

Eye contact

Making eye contact for about two-thirds of the time is usually about right for a comfortable conversation, but judge this for yourself. Women tend to use eye contact a little more than men do. Avoid staring constantly; this doesn't show deep interest as is sometimes thought. It is more likely to appear a little aggressive, and is very off-putting. Similarly, if you look away too much, this can make you seem uninterested or distracted. So on a first meeting with someone, as a very rough guide, look for 3–4 seconds, then glance away for 1–2 seconds, then look back for another 3–4 seconds, and so on.

Tone of voice

Almost as important as your body language is your voice and how you use it. Body language and tone of voice together convey most of what we communicate to others. Aim for a warm, gentle, low-pitched and friendly tone, in tune with what is being said to you.

Building trust

If you find it difficult to make and keep friends, it can make you overly eager in the friendship arena. This can mean that as soon as you have got to the early stages of a new friendship or with a new partner, you simply can't wait to make it a closer relationship by sharing too much of yourself too early.

Unfortunately, what this is most likely to do is scare the other person off, and you've failed again. Or the person won't know how to react to your perhaps over-enthusiastic approach, and will probably say that what you feel is the wrong thing, so that you maybe feel hurt or offended. Then you have problems with the relationship, and you won't really understand what went wrong. You'll blame yourself again, and your faith in human nature will be reduced yet again.

To break this painful and discouraging cycle, you have to go at the 'accepted' pace with new relationships, and build trust and intimacy slowly but surely, one tentative and measured step at a time. Yes, this takes patience, but it is worth it. You'll be much more successful in keeping new friends, until they become that wonderful and most precious of things, an old friend. There are some things in life that you just can't rush, and making a strong and lasting relationship is one of them.

And to finish – take it slowly

Don't go overboard on everything we've covered in this chapter – you'll become too distracted, and possibly confused! Concentrate on changing just one thing at a time. Step by step is the surest way to make and maintain good progress. And as is said often, the longest of journeys begins with a single step. You can always refer back to this book regularly for more ideas, once you've mastered a few main changes. So, where are you going to start? Keep this at the back of your mind as you read on, and in Chapter 12, I'll come back to helping you to work this out, and take things forward carefully and gradually.

5

Coping with stimulus and regaining a sense of control

An important place to start is in your own head! Why? Because over many years of being sensitive and coping with that in every area of your life, you can begin to feel that you are not in control of your life. What you do, or don't do each day, what sort of mood you find yourself in, the thoughts that are going through your head, all these seem to be under the control of other people rather than under yours. What happened at work yesterday, how you got on with your partner over dinner last night, the way your neighbour greeted you this morning, all of these can seem to dictate your life. So much seems to be going on, and it can all feel overwhelming. Even the loud music in shops and the crowds on the train can be just too much to bear: too much stimulation for an already vulnerable and over-reacting nervous system.

Redressing the balance

Before you can begin to raise your confidence, and be sure of who you are again, we have to get this right, and give you back control of your life. Of course we can't control everything that happens to us, and how we're going to react to things each day, but we do need to redress the balance a bit. You need to feel that you do have at least some say in your life – and obviously, the more, the better!

This may seem like a lot to ask for, but is actually a lot easier than it sounds. First, let me tell you about two women I know, Joanna and Pamela, who are cousins living in the same city in the north of England.

Joanna C.
Joanna lives in a very nice detached house on the edge of the city. For as long as she can remember she has lacked confidence in herself, and has been plagued by mood swings. Not the kind of mood swings you need treatment for, just general ups and downs in her confidence in herself. Her two daughters are now teenagers, and she hopes they won't have the problems she's had. Things can be going fine and she feels her confidence growing, but then she has a problem with someone – a neighbour, a friend, someone

45

at work, or even her husband Graham. Then she feels her mood and her self-esteem taking a nosedive again. Her neighbour may have complained about the girls playing their music too loud. Her boss might have told her that she wasn't meeting her targets. The girls may have moaned because she wouldn't increase their pocket money. Or Graham hadn't taken her out anywhere nice for a while. Her mood is all right when everything is going well, but something always seems to be going wrong and making her feel bad.

What's going on here? This is an everyday story of an ordinary family, and yet Joanna is unhappy, and has low self-esteem. The problem is that how Joanna sees herself seems to be dictated by the circumstances and people around her. What people think of her, or appear to think of her on any one day, has a profound influence on how she feels about herself.

Let's just replay the situation this time for Joanna's cousin Pamela, who lives nearby.

Pamela R.

Pamela lives a few streets away from Joanna. Their lives are very similar, but Pamela is one of those people who always seem to be cheerful. Pamela enjoys life and enjoys going out with friends. Her neighbour, Maria, recently asked her if she could cut back an overgrown bush, which was cutting out the sun from her garden. She agreed to do so and then asked Maria to pop in for a coffee that afternoon, when she had finished it. She just hadn't got round to pruning that bush because the weather had been bad for weeks. At work next day, her manager raised the subject of her being behind with her work targets, and Pamela explained that she'd had a very busy few weeks, but she would catch up next month. They had been particularly busy with new clients this month, making it difficult to meet all the deadlines. Pamela's husband, Jerry, had been a bit overtired recently, so they hadn't been out for a while together. So before she left work, she phoned to book his favourite restaurant as a treat for that evening for the two of them.

Another story of everyday people. But a very different one. Could you see what was making the difference? The background circumstances were all very similar. What was different was how the two women made sense of what was going on around them, and their role in it all.

People divide into two camps in how they make sense of the world. Which camp we are in is usually decided by a combination of our genes and our upbringing. One camp largely gains their sense of self from how others behave towards them. That is, their sense of who they are and the causes of what happens to them is all down to external factors over which they have little control. This is how Joanna sees the world. How she feels about herself today is largely down to what the last person she spoke to seemed to think about her, or what the last thing which happened in her life was. It's easy to see that this way of looking at life tends to cause low self-image, and in turn poor self-confidence.

Pamela belongs to the other camp. People in this camp have a strong and unshakeable sense of self-worth and identity lying deep within themselves, and this does not alter no matter what anyone thinks of them, or what goes wrong in their lives. They can see that most often things that go wrong are caused by other factors, and not by them. They are also aware that they have some control over their lives, and can do something about problems. Pamela has an internal sense of who she is, and knows that she herself can exert control over what goes on around her. Again it's easy to see that such a view of life tends to maintain self-worth and confidence.

Which camp do you feel you belong to? If you see the world a bit like Joanna does, you are not the only one. But you can change this attitude. Becoming aware of it is the first and most important step. So you've taken that one already. The other step is gaining a strong and positive sense of who you are, which doesn't depend on what other people think or say about you, and doesn't depend on the friends you have at the time. That's what we have been doing already in this book, and we will continue to work on that.

The personality with a sense of control

A psychologist named Suzanne Kobasa includes a sense of control in her idea of a 'hardy personality', in relation to stress. Control seems to be a vital issue in any discussion about stress. Intuitively, it seems right that faced with a threatening or difficult situation over which we feel we have no control, stress is likely to be that much greater than if we feel there is something we can do about it. I'm sure this is a feeling you can relate to, all too well.

But sometimes awareness of whether or not we have control is less clear-cut than we might think. I will now introduce you to Kevin and Liz:

Kevin P.

Kevin is 19, and has just begun a course in biochemistry at a large university, and is finding it increasingly difficult to cope with the work. The lectures are complicated, and the pace is faster than he expected. It's difficult to get to know people as the lectures have so many people in them. After only six weeks, he feels that the work is totally out of his control, and that he just isn't up to it. He's also been feeling panicky and light-headed during lectures, and has had to leave the lecture for some fresh air on several occasions. He's sure he'll have to give up at Christmas, and is angry that life isn't fair. Why do these things always happen to him?

Liz T.

Liz is also 19, and on the same course as Kevin. She has noticed him having to go out of the room during lectures. She found the sudden increase in pace and level a shock at first, but decided she would need to put in more study to keep up, and that seemed to work. She also made a point of talking to other students, and discovered they all felt the same. She finds the library helpful to find books on the parts of the course she finds difficult to understand, and the tutorials are very useful for asking questions. She's confident she can cope with the course and is enjoying the experience.

As early as 1966, J. B. Rotter was describing the significance of people's perception of whether or not they have control over situations. He introduced the concept of 'locus of control'. 'Locus' just means where something is. You may have heard police officers talk about the 'locus' of a crime, and they simply mean where the crime took place. So 'locus of control' is just another way of saying where control lies. So Rotter would describe Kevin as having an 'external locus of control', and Liz, an 'internal locus of control'.

That is, Liz feels she has her own, internal control over what happens to her, and that her actions and decisions have an effect on her life experience. So she works harder, finds out how others are feeling, and gets further help from the library. Kevin, on the other hand, feels he has little influence or control over events, and that external factors such as fate or chance are largely responsible for what happens to him. So he sits back and takes whatever happens to him as if he has no power to alter it. A kind of 'learned helplessness'. Kevin is therefore likely to experience stress and anxiety, whilst Liz is not. Remember Joanne and Pamela earlier in this chapter? Which has an 'internal' and which an 'external' locus of control? Yes, Joanne's is probably 'internal', and Pamela's is probably 'external'.

Rotter's view was that those with an external locus of control are more vulnerable to stress, anxiety and worrying in most situations. Such people tend to hold some or all of the following beliefs – what about you?

- Luck and chance play a crucial role in life.
- Success is determined by being in the right place at the right time.
- What happens to us is pre-destined.
- It really matters what people think or say about me.
- In our lives, we are all subject to forces which we cannot control.

It is probably worth saying that the issue of control may be one which arises from life in a culture in which much of our daily life is unpredictable and outside our control. It could all be so different in a different kind of world.

The role of anticipation and imagination

An important common thread running through this book is the ability of human beings to anticipate and imagine the future. We are probably quite alone in the animal kingdom in having these abilities.

There is, however, a down side to being able to think about the future. This unique ability lies at the heart of problems with being sensitive. If we couldn't think about what might happen, if we couldn't visualize the possible consequences of our situation, we would be blissfully unaware of them. So stress, worry and anxiety form a price we pay for being a very sophisticated animal mentally. And the more imaginative and creative we are about our own possible future, the more we may find we have a capacity to worry about this. For example, we can imagine all too clearly what our friends will say if we fail our driving test. We can clearly picture the consequences if we don't get that project at work finished on time. And we can conjure up a surprisingly long list of what can possibly go wrong next!

Where control really lies

Of course control in our lives doesn't actually lie either outside us or inside us. It's somewhere in between these two for most of us, most of the time.

What usually happens to us is a mixture of the effects of what is happening externally, and how we react to this within ourselves, or internally. If you know there is an exam coming up, you know you are capable of a pass, you study for it, and achieve a reasonable pass on the day.

Sometimes it's all down to external factors. If you are sunbathing on the beach, and the rain suddenly pours down despite a weather forecast predicting good weather, you will get wet and be disappointed. You have no say in such matters. On the other hand, it can all be down to 'internal' factors. You may know you have an exam coming up, but you are so worried that you'll fail that you can't concentrate on studying, and you panic on the day of the exam. You fail the exam, reinforcing your feelings of inadequacy.

Making friends and finding a partner

Sometimes, you can find it easier to get your sense of who you are from your partner or friends. This can seem fine if all is going well. But what happens when your relationship with your partner breaks down, or your friends move away? You can find yourself feeling very lost and alone, and not sure who you are again. In other words your self-esteem and identity are controlled and defined by your current relationships. And if certain people disappear from your life, your identity goes too. This is a very vulnerable way to live, with control over your identity lying outside of you and in other people's hands. You don't want to live like that, so take on board everything in the book about building up your own identity and self-worth, and keeping this inside yourself where it is safe and secure.

Taking all this together, aim to really believe you can affect what happens in your life, and that you can exert control from within yourself to counteract external factors. Believe that you are too sure of who you are, and too grounded, to be deeply affected by how people react or don't react to you. There is only one you, and there will never be another one again. Don't just resign yourself to what happens out there, outside of you.

Coping with people in authority

Sometimes, people who represent authority can be particularly daunting or even intimidating. As with so many situations, every-thing you read in this book will help you to cope with this more effectively. However, here are ten ideas which may make this easier to deal with:

1 imagine the person or people in authority are in their underwear, in the nude, or better still, on the toilet – this helps to make them seem more human, and on a more equal footing with you;
2 imagine the person or people in authority wearing silly fancy dress costumes – a large pink rabbit with floppy ears can be particularly helpful;
3 have a list of your questions ready;
4 don't be afraid to have some notes – the person in authority will have some, so you can too;
5 be sure of your facts – do a bit of research first if necessary;
6 know your rights in the situation – check them out before-hand;
7 take a friend or other appropriate person along if you can for support;
8 keep a 'good' attitude – pleasant, friendly, warm, assertive (see Chapter 7 for more details);
9 keep to your main points – don't be distracted from them;
10 be prepared to go higher up if necessary.

Getting back in the driving seat

Part of being sensitive, then, is that you may not feel in control of your life. I wonder if this has come as a surprise to you. It often does. Most people are simply not aware of this going on inside their heads every day. But it's so nice to find out, and then be able to do something to change this, and make things better.

Feeling that you have no say in your life leads to all sorts of the problems we've talked about already – frustration, stress, anxiety, worry, tension, moods, and so on. Then of course these can make you feel even more sensitive, and so on – a sort of self-fulfilling prophecy and vicious circle, all in one.

How are you going to turn this around and regain that control? How can you get out of the passenger seat, and back into the driving seat of life? Here's how what has already been discussed in this book, and what is yet to come, will help with this.

Already covered in earlier chapters:

Understanding and awareness about 'control' is half the battle.
Remember all the positive sides to being sensitive – make these work for you every day.
Forgive yourself for being sensitive – it's not your fault.
Remember you have the right to exert control in a situation.

Remember you are a unique and special person.

Grow to like and respect yourself.

Grow a positive and unshakeable sense of identity and self-esteem.

Later chapters will cover:

How to cope better with moods and mood swings.

Coping better with anger.

How to be more assertive.

Using your voice to express yourself better.

How to relax your nervous system, mind and body.

How to make your thinking processes work better for you.

How to plan and take action.

6

Coping with mood swings

If you are over-sensitive, you may well be more vulnerable to moodiness and mood swings. Events that others might not even notice may be upsetting, leaving you worried, angry or even in tears. We've already seen how you may be troubled by a tendency to over-react or take offence. We've also considered how being too sensitive has related problems such as disturbed sleep, negativity, disappointment, exhaustion, frustration, depression, and anxiety. All such aspects of sensitivity can make you more prone to moods, arguments and upsets.

Everything in this book should help you to become more at ease with yourself and reduce moodiness. We've already helped you to understand more about sensitivity, and demonstrated its positive side, and explained how you can build up your confidence in yourself. Later chapters will suggest exercises to help you to relax your body and your mind, and become more assertive. In this chapter we will look in detail at the mood swings themselves, and I'll show you how to lessen these.

Here are just some of the problems being moody can bring. I'm sure these come as no surprise to you. But remember you're not alone – and you can do a lot to improve matters.

Being moody can cause:

Worry
Anxiety
Tearfulness
Rapid mood changes – up one minute, down the next
Longer downs
Tension
Relationship problems
Constant rows and arguments
Anger, aggression and frustration
Depression
Guilt
A feeling that nobody understands
Introversion
Self-imposed isolation
Never knowing where you are

Self-dislike
Sudden outbursts
Regret
Violence, physical or mental, with, for example, damage to property or to relationships

Reasons for being moody

But why are you moody? Could there be more to it than just being sensitive? Let's look at some other possible reasons for your moods. Most of these are relevant only to women; some may apply to men too. Any or all of these other causes of moodiness may be affecting you over and above your being sensitive, giving a sort of doubling or even trebling of the effect. So it's well worth tackling these too.

Before a period

Don't listen to any of those media and expert reports which say that pre-menstrual syndrome (PMS) doesn't exist. It does, and it can have a very powerful effect on your moods, such as feeling low, very sudden mood swings, outbursts of anger, and irrational thinking. Many an argument happens at this time of the month. There is much you can do to help yourself. Key are staying fit and eating a healthy balanced diet, as certain key vitamins and your blood sugar levels seem to have a major impact on PMS (more on this on pages 55–6). Do try these simple strategies first, and speak to your doctor if self-help measures don't seem to be working. It is helpful if you keep a diary of your behaviour, moods and other symptoms such as bloating, breast tenderness and cravings, for a few months before you visit your doctor, who may be able to prescribe medication.

After a baby

Likewise, after having a baby, your hormones can be all over the place, and will take time to settle back to normal after the upheaval of pregnancy and breastfeeding. You'll also be even more tired than usual, unless you are very lucky! This can all mean that your moods are volatile, with tears never very far away. For some, post-natal depression is a possibility, so if your mood is consistently very low after your baby is born, do have a word with your GP, who should be able to help you. (See pages 58–9 where I give some more guidance on dealing with depression.)

The menopause and perimenopause

Yes, those hormones again! The years running up to the menopause, when periods stop, are called the perimenopause, during which time you may again be subject to mood swings. You may also find that PMS becomes more severe during this time, or you may experience it for the first time. Periods which are heavier than normal, or irregular and unpredictable, can also leave you feeling on edge, upset and moody. Rest assured that you are not alone, and, as before, if this is getting too difficult to cope with, ask your GP for help. Some people find it easier to make an appointment with a female doctor.

Mid-life crises (women and men)

When we reach late 30s or early 40s, many of us begin to question what life is all about, and where we are going. Some people become acutely aware of ambitions unrealized, and may feel that others appear to be doing much better in the race that is today's life. What has been achieved so far? Is it too late to achieve anything else?

Bereavement is often part of growing older. You may lose your parents or your partner and may feel there is nothing standing between you and the end of your life. This can leave you feeling scared, vulnerable and lost. Don't be afraid to talk these feelings out with a trusted friend or adviser, such as a life coach.

What you can do

Is there anything that can be done about all these moods and related problems? Yes, of course. But it does take work. You'll have to draw yourself up when you're in a mood, and do something different from what the mood is dictating! Sometimes, that's much easier said than done. So here are some coping strategies to help you and your nearest and dearest to survive your moods.

Understanding your moods

Just understanding why you are feeling the way you do can have an amazingly calming effect. It can release you from your self-imposed guilt. It can also help if your friends, colleagues and partner can understand better too. So, explain it to them on a good day, or let them read this book.

How your diet can help

You're probably tired of being told to eat a healthy diet. But, sorry, here it is again. Eating a healthy and well-balanced diet can really help your moods. But be careful to keep the balance right. There is evidence to suggest that eating a diet which is too low in fat may lead to low mood, or even depression.

Often, one of the main reasons people become angry, apparently out of the blue is because their blood sugar level is low. Eat small and healthy regular meals, avoiding refined sugar products – no skipping breakfast, and then filling up on a chocolate bar or chocolate biscuit for elevenses. This will just give you a high, followed by a sudden dip, and that's the danger time for an outburst of anger.

Exercise

Again, you're probably fed up with being told to take exercise, but it's true that, taken regularly, it does help even out those mood swings. It also improves mood generally, as the brain physiology which exercise produces makes you feel good. It's also great for working off feelings of frustration, anger and tension safely. The secret is to choose a form of exercise which you enjoy, as you are much more likely to keep it up.

Coping with anger and arguments

Frustration brought on by sensitivity may build and build, until one day, for no particular reason, it may suddenly explode into anger, a tantrum, or even into violence, occasionally leading people into actions which they may later regret. For others, simmering anger may surface in the form of frequent verbal or even physical aggression.

Sometimes this anger does not escape at all, but stays deep inside, producing a feeling of despair or depression, which may be experienced as a physical feeling of a weight on the chest. Depression will be discussed later in this chapter, but, for now, let me stress that it's important to talk to your doctor straightaway if you feel you are having difficulties with depression.

It can sometimes be more acceptable for a man to show anger than a woman, making suppressed anger, and possible depression, likely to be more of a problem for women. Men often have an outlet for such feelings via a contact sport such as rugby or football. Women are expected to be warm, nurturing and caring, and even small deviations from this can be frowned upon, misconstrued and misrepresented.

Other unhelpful ways of dealing with internal frustration and anger are to eat too much or too little, drink or smoke too much, use drugs (prescribed or otherwise), or to withdraw emotionally or physically from life. All of these have other consequences in terms of our physical and mental well-being.

It is crucial to do something about angry feelings. They can't just be left to sort themselves out. Chapter 7 on assertiveness will give you more help with not becoming angry in the first place, but here are some practical suggestions on how to let anger out safely, instead of bottling it all up.

If you can, leave the room or situation and:

1 go for a brisk walk or run outside, until you can remember the good things of life;
2 release the energy constructively by doing something physically demanding and useful, like gardening, aerobics, or cleaning.

Or leave the room or situation, find somewhere private and:

1 take a deep breath and yell 'I hate everyone!', then take another deep breath and let it out with a quiet, 'Now I feel better and I'm ready to like people again';
2 shout your feelings out to an inanimate object – stuffed toy, plant, anything;
3 punch an inanimate object such as a cushion, pillow, stuffed toy or even a punch bag bought for the purpose;
4 tear up old papers or magazines, expressing your angry thoughts at the same time – it saves buying a shredder;
5 cry if you want to;
6 stamp your feet and shout;
7 shout or say loudly 'I'm angry!' or 'No, no, no!!'
8 if you can't find somewhere suitable to make loud noises, find a private corner (the loo perhaps?) and mutter any of the above suggestions under your breath over and over until you feel better.

To release more long-term anger

1 Write an angry poem or draw an angry picture (not for others' viewing). Keep it or tear it up.
2 Write down your angry thoughts. Keep these or tear them up. (Again, this is just for your eyes – don't let anyone see these unless you want to show them.)

3 Write it all down in an angry letter to the person you are angry with (tear up the letter afterwards, or keep it somewhere safe).
4 Pretend the person you are angry with is in an empty chair, and tell him or her why you are so angry.

Importance of social support

Having someone to talk to can be such a help. Friends, family or a partner can be really effective in helping you create a 'cushion' against the daily hassles and stresses of life as a sensitive person. All of us need positive social support, but this can be even more important to the sensitive person. Having someone who cares about us, and who is interested in what we do, is a big stress-reliever, and can also prevent some mood problems arising in the first place. So if you have a good support system, make maximum use of it. No need to feel guilty for doing this. You can always repay the favour.

Make a start today – look back at the suggestions on making good friends in Chapter 4.

Relaxation and work–life balance

Later chapters will help you with relaxation, and this can make all the difference. You should also make sure that your life is balanced between work-time and time for you and your life. You only have one life, so make sure that you take the time to live it and experience every second of it.

Coping with depression

People often use the word *depressed* as a sort of throw-away comment.

'I'm feeling really depressed about my car. It's always breaking down.' Or, 'This weather is so depressing.' Maybe they are genuinely depressed. But it is much more likely that they are simply a bit fed up, a perfectly reasonable reaction, which we can all experience for a day or so, from time to time.

If however you have been having problems with your sensitivity for some time, persisting low mood may result. This can vary from occasionally feeling down, to a deeper and more long-lasting experience of feeling very low, weepy and despairing. This is true depression, and is a much more serious and distressing affair. Lasting more than just a few days, it involves low mood, and long tearful episodes. Other signs are persistent feelings of hopelessness, despair and anxiety, lack of energy, poor appetite, and difficulty sleeping, especially waking early in the morning. The first and most important thing you should do if you think you might be depressed, is to go along and a have a chat with your doctor.

Of course, all of this may happen the other way around. Sometimes, if you are depressed, you can find that you feel very touchy, sensitive, moody and weepy. It can sometimes be difficult to work out which came first, the depression or the sensitivity.

Possibilities for medical or counselling input

This chapter has dealt with a variety of conditions and reasons for being moody. If you find that despite reading this book and trying some of the self-help ideas given, you are still having difficulties with your mood, then it's always worth having a chat with your doctor about this. Further straightforward help such as medication or specialist therapy or counselling should then be available to you.

7

Sensitive steps towards assertion

We're now going to look a much misunderstood topic, assertiveness. This is definitely not about being self-centred and aggressive, as is sometimes thought. Nor does it mean you having to stand up to unpleasant people, or make a fuss – just what you'd rather not do.

The idea of assertiveness came over from the USA in the 1960s, with a huge impact made by Anne Dickson's ground-breaking book on the subject (*A Woman in Your Own Right: Assertivness and You*, London, Quartet Books, 1982). Assertiveness is based on the view that everyone is equal, and has the same rights, and that we should have respect for ourselves and each other.

Assertiveness is not about being aggressive. It's about being able to express your needs and views in a calm, effective manner, and in a way which respects both you and the other person/s involved. It is simply the ability to deal with others in a calm, confident and effective way. This clearly has a lot to do with sensitivity. In fact, it's just what you need! Aggressive people ignore the needs and rights of other people. The sensitive person is always thinking about them. This puts you in a good position to work from, and make your sensitivity work for you.

By making your behaviour more assertive, you may be able to change a difficult situation into one that can be managed, and prevent other difficult situations from arising at all. What then does it mean to be assertive? Here is a list of points:

- knowing your own needs and rights;
- being aware of other people's needs and rights;
- having genuine respect for yourself;
- having genuine respect for others;
- being open, direct and honest whenever appropriate;
- being able to compromise.

Sounds simple, doesn't it? But it can be hard going to achieve this in the real world, especially if you have baggage from the past which undermines your image of yourself. Habits of a lifetime take a little bit of time to change. But it can be done.

You may find that you often behave much more passively than this. Do any of these apply to you?

- Dropping hints.
- Making excuses.
- Unable to say 'no'.
- The dogsbody.
- Difficulty making decisions.
- Apologizing all the time.
- Putting everyone else first all the time.
- Holding anger in, and then maybe letting it out by losing your temper.

In your dealings with other people, do you find they do any of these things *to you*?

- Get their own way by making you feel guilty.
- Use sarcasm to you.
- Put you down.
- Sulk and not speak to you.
- Shout at you.
- Scare, dominate or threaten you.
- Are not there for you, though you are for them.
- Have to be right all the time.

This last list describes some of the ways in which non-assertive people might behave towards you. They are not thinking about you and your needs. They are simply thinking of their own. The over-sensitive person may be an easy target for this, and people get to know this. If you make any changes, it's best to make them slowly and carefully, almost by stealth, so that no one even notices. Except you, of course.

Making a start

It may surprise you to find out that in this book, we have already made quite a start on assertiveness skills! By working on aspects of your life such as anger, mood swings, body language, confidence, and control, you also make improvements on how assertive you are. Still not sure? Let's explain a bit more about assertiveness.

People who are sensitive often find it difficult to be assertive, usually due to a deeply felt lack of self-respect. Sometimes they may be so used to feeling this way that they may not even have been aware of it. They may even have felt that this lack of respect was justified. If you have felt like that, I hope that this book has already taken you some way towards changing that view of yourself, especially in Chapter 4, where we looked at how you see yourself, and what is important to you.

Lack of assertiveness, then, has a major impact on our own behaviour and on our dealings with the great variety of the people we meet every day. How can this be changed?

Angela S.

Angela was 54, and for the past ten years had been expected to look after her widowed mother, who was 78 and had a heart condition. Even though Angela had a sister, Elizabeth, Angela was always the one who was called at work if there was anything wrong. She also had to do her mother's shopping every week. She just couldn't bring herself to ask Elizabeth to help her, as she didn't want to upset her or quarrel with her. Angela found she was neglecting her own family – her husband Eric, and two sons, Mark and Gary. She was feeling drained, tense, and agitated, starting at the slightest noise. She couldn't relax, and felt depressed and frustrated.

Dev P.

Dev worked in a large pharmaceutical company, in the marketing department. He used to really enjoy his work, but due to downsizing, his line manager changed. He felt his new manager was overseeing him all the time, and never seemed happy with his work. Dev never had this problem before. His previous manager was always happy with his work, so he felt demoralized and worried by all this criticism.

Angela had slipped into the habit of being her mother's principal carer, and others accepted this, as they tend to do, being busy with their own lives. Maybe she couldn't say 'no' ten years ago when her father died, and was now stuck with the consequences. This can happen all too easily. Angela needed to be able to make changes in a slow and careful way, which she herself could cope with, and that other people could accept, without even noticing it. She needed to work slowly towards her responsibilities being shared around a bit more. She could then take control of her life.

Dev was having a problem dealing with a leaner marketing department, where his manager had to get more work out of fewer staff. He had never been criticized before, and was finding this hard to deal with. But none of us is perfect, and criticism can be an everyday part of working life. If Dev could improve his self-worth and have enough faith in himself and his own abilities to take criticism without feeling devalued, he could begin to respect himself again and enjoy his work once more. But how to do this?

Body language

Being assertive begins with the impression you make with your body and behaviour. Before we think about the sort of things assertive people say, and how to deal with criticism, do remember the silent language which speaks volumes about us: our body language. We've already talked a bit about body language when we covered building your confidence in Chapter 4. Everything we said there, applies here too, so have a quick look back now if you need to refresh your memory.

Learning how to say 'no'

One of the most common difficulties about being assertive is being unable to say 'no' to people. If you have a tendency to passivity, then you may find it a problem to say 'no' to friends, partner, colleagues or family. This is all down to putting their needs before yours, instead of realizing that your needs are of the same importance as theirs, and on some occasions, more important.

Constantly saying 'yes' when you want to say 'no' to requests to do a favour, change your plans, lend something, or whatever, simply stokes the boiler of frustration and can lead to anger in the longer term. This anger can eventually be turned on those same people, or on yourself. You can also become overworked and overloaded because you've taken on more than you can comfortably cope with.

Think about how often other people say 'no' to you. You probably just accept this, and don't get offended, so why should they get offended if you behave in the same way? Saying 'no' when you want to is an important skill to practise. We're not talking about being selfish. There will be times when you decide that you want to say 'yes', even though it might be inconvenient. Remember, assertiveness means respecting both your needs and rights, and those of others, and compromising when necessary.

Below are some suggestions for how to say 'no'. As with the other ideas in this book, avoid making too many changes in your behaviour at once. Trying to change too much will confuse you, and be difficult to sustain. In particular, saying no may come as a surprise to others, and you may need to repeat it in some situations.

Try these out slowly to begin with, and in less important situations:

Take your time before you answer

A key tip is to allow a second or two to think before you reply to someone's request, as you may find that the words 'OK' or 'yes' slip out automatically, before you have time to think.

Body language when you say 'no'

With most of these techniques, you should slow down, speak steadily and with warmth, otherwise you can sound overly abrupt. Practise it in the mirror or into an audio or video recorder. Or ask a trusted friend how it sounds. It's certainly worth getting used to hearing the word 'NO' coming out of your mouth.

Broken record

It is often important to be able to persist with saying 'no', as people are likely to try to make you change your mind. Children can be particularly good at this! A useful technique is to 'broken record' your refusal, by simply parroting it back quietly and calmly, no matter what pressure the other person puts upon you.

Don't over-apologize

The aim here is not to apologize unless it is appropriate to do so. If you lack confidence in yourself, you may find that you say you're sorry a lot! So don't begin sentences with 'I'm sorry . . .', or 'I'm afraid . . .'. The other person may have a problem, but you don't have to allow them to give it to you. So you might say:

'No, I don't want new double-glazing.'
'No, I'd prefer not to take your catalogue.'
'No, I'd rather not buy a raffle ticket.'

Keep it short

Avoid long rambling explanations of why you can't say 'Yes'. So don't say things like, 'I wouldn't normally say 'no', and I hope you don't mind, but I have friends coming in from Outer Mongolia, and . . .'

These short phrases are useful for saying 'no', but must be said with warmth:

'I'd rather not.'
'I don't have time.'
'I don't want to.'
'I just can't manage it today.'

Reflecting

Here you reflect back the content and feeling of what is being asked of you, but end with a refusal to meet the request.

'No, I can't help you with the garden this afternoon.'

'But I'd really looked forward to starting it.'

'I realize you were looking forward to it, but I can't help you this afternoon.'

(Reflection)

'I've got to get it finished this weekend.'

'I know you've got to finish it this weekend, but I can't help you this afternoon.'

(Reflection and broken record)

Reasoned 'no'

This gives very briefly, the genuine reason for the 'no'. But only give a reason if you want to or need to. You don't have to explain yourself to every Tom, Dick and Harry who makes demands of you.

'I can't help you with your report today, because I have a meeting all afternoon.'

'I haven't got time, because I have to collect the children from school.'

The raincheck 'no'

This says 'no' for just now, but leaves room for negotiation.

'I can't help you this weekend, because I'm working, but I might be able to find a bit of time next weekend.'

Asking for information

This is not a definite 'no', but leaves room for a compromise, or a later 'no':

'Why do you need it done this afternoon?'

'How much detail would the report need?'

'Could you get started on it without me?'

Asking for time to decide

Never be afraid just to ask for some time to think.

'I just need to check my work schedule, then I'll get back to you.'

'I'm not really sure just now. Can I ring you back later?'

Choosing which way to say 'no'

The particular technique you use will of course depend on the situation, and how you judge it. These may range from a persistent salesperson, to a neighbour who expects too much of you, to a friend you'd like to help, but just can't on that occasion. A straight 'no' is the most uncompromising. Remember, you don't owe everybody an explanation! A reflection is probably the most understanding as it shows you've listened to the other person. Asking for information or giving a raincheck 'no' leaves open the possibility of continued negotiation. You can also combine techniques to meet the needs of the situation.

Handling criticism

We all make mistakes, and this does have many positive aspects – we learn a great deal. But criticism can be one of the hardest things to cope with in an assertive way, especially if we lack confidence. It feels a bit like being kicked when you're already down. But we hope that you've already made some progress from being 'down'. We hope that you've begun to improve your feelings of worth and self-esteem, and begun to know who you are and develop a positive self-image that comes from inside you. This will of course take time, and you've only just made a start. But in time, all of these changes will help you to cope better with criticism, because you'll be responding on a more level playing field than you were before.

When you lack confidence in yourself, you will often accept unfair criticism or straightforward insults, and take it very much to heart. This will undermine your confidence still further. When you are sensitive, even the smallest criticism can be so painful and demoralizing, and prey on your mind for days, and can even make you lose sleep worrying about it. Again, we hope that this book has helped you to be much more aware of your skills and talents, and your strengths, making it easier to be able to know the difference between criticism which is realistic and fair comment, and criticism or insults which are unfair, unreasonable and unfounded. Yes, there is a difference! Just because someone says it, doesn't make it true.

Let's look now at some assertive ways to respond to both of these types of criticism. But first you have to get used to being able to tell the difference, and not just assume that all criticism is fair. Think about it. Allow yourself to get to know who you are, and grow and nurture a solid sense of a positive self. You are a good, kind and

caring person – you wouldn't be reading this book if you weren't!
No one has the right to insult you or criticize you unfairly.

Coping with fair criticism

Accept it

The simplest response is to accept the criticism without expressing
guilt or making an apology. We all make mistakes, and the best
thing is to hold your hand up to it, correct the situation, and learn
from it. It has been said that the person who never made a mistake,
never did anything.

'You didn't make a very good job of that.'

'No, I didn't, did I? I'll have to have another go at it.'

Ask for information

Another way of coping is to accept the criticism but ask for more
information about it from the person doing the criticizing.

'You didn't clean the flat very well.'

'No, it wasn't too good, was it? Was it the hoovering or was it the
bathroom that was the main problem?'

Coping with unfair criticism or insults

Disagree with it

Calmly and assertively disagree:

'You're always late for meetings.'

'No, I'm not always late. I may have been late once or twice, but
I'm definitely not always late.'

Ask for information

You can use this technique to accept the criticism, but also continue
to ask for more information (as above) until the criticizer wishes he
or she hadn't raised the subject!

Use fogging

Once again, fogging can be really helpful. Fog the issue, giving the
criticizer nothing substantial to get a hold on. You can use phrases
like:

'Perhaps you are right . . .'

'Sometimes I can be . . .'

'You could be right . . .'

'There could be some truth in that . . .'

So the criticism seems to be accepted, but is actually having little impact. This will also put the criticizer off criticizing you unfairly again.

Take change step by step

I've already said it, but it's worth repeating. This book is just a starting point. What we're suggesting is a new way of life for you. There is a great deal for you to put into practice, and this will take time. So don't expect overnight miracles, and don't rush at everything all at once. Start small, and build up gradually, almost so no one notices. Just work at it slowly but surely, and you should soon reap the benefits. This book is not just for reading through once. You can look back over it any time you need to refresh your memory, or pick out what you feel are the most important ideas and techniques for you. And in the final chapter, we'll get you to put together an overall 'Personal Action Plan' to work on, which should help to keep you on track.

Remember, don't try to make too many changes at once. Change is stressful in itself and it's very difficult to sustain too many changes all at the same time. So take your time, and make sure that you've achieved one change before moving on to the next. The 'softly softly' approach is most likely to succeed in the long term.

Summary of assertiveness tips

- Value yourself.
- Value other people.
- Know what you need or want.
- Be prepared to compromise.
- Speak confidently: slow, steady, low-pitched and warm.
- Stand or sit confidently: head up, direct eye contact.
- Calmly repeat your request if necessary.
- Keep to your point – don't be distracted from it.
- Say 'no' when you want or need to.
- Always start small, and with the less important situations.

8

Calming your sensitivity 1: physical tips

Too much sustained tension brought on by being sensitive can make you feel quite ill. You may find that you have symptoms such as headaches, digestive upsets, back pain, fatigue, dizziness, or just vague aches and pains and general malaise which you can't quite put your finger on. This may even have happened to you as a child with frequent tummy upsets, aches, pains or fatigue, keeping you off school. It's easy to see how all this can take over your life.

By far the best way to tackle tension is through relaxing regularly, and that means every day. This will help to reduce the feelings of tension, anxiety and frustration which being sensitive can bring. Relaxing for at least a short period every day has the added benefit of 'damping down' your body's tendency to become tense in the first place.

These are very good reasons for making an early start and learning this important skill. For many people the straightforward answer to this is to spend time regularly on an activity which reduces tension in the muscles.

There are all sorts of ways to do this. It's down to your preferences. The important thing is that you allow your body to slow down and completely relax at least once every day. A walk on the beach, a lazy bath, listening to music, yoga, gardening, physical activity such as swimming or jogging, and so on, can all be relaxing depending on your own individual taste. The key thing is to take time out to do something you enjoy and which is relaxing for you. It is sometimes useful to join a relaxation group in your area, especially if it's hard to get the time and space at home. Yoga classes are another option, as they usually end with a long and most enjoyable relaxation session.

If your time is tight, you may think that taking time to do this will just get you even further behind, but this is not the case. If your body is allowed to relax regularly, you will actually be able to get more done more effectively with the time left, because you will be refreshed and energized.

But, while everyday simple measures are the first avenue to try, there can be a number of drawbacks with this kind of approach to relaxation, particularly for severe or long-lasting tension.

- Tension may be so persistent that your muscles need to be relaxed frequently, several times a day or more.
- You may be so tense that this kind of approach just doesn't work.
- Tension often occurs whilst doing something else, such as in the workplace.
- You may not be able to find an everyday activity which relaxes you.
- Most of these activities are quite time-consuming.
- You may have been so tense for so long that you've forgotten how to relax.

We all come into this world able to relax. Think of the dead weight of a sleeping baby or toddler. But you can lose this skill very easily. You may have to relearn it, and if so, you will probably need to practise it to become good at it again. Just like learning any new skill, you have to practise. Imagine trying to ride a bike, play the piano or drive a car without having practised first.

It often requires more specialist techniques than simple everyday activities, to really get to grips with physical and mental tension. Simple, non-strenuous relaxation exercises are the easiest and most convenient. Don't be put off, if you've tried relaxation exercises before and it didn't work – if it didn't work you were doing it wrong, so give it another chance!

Relaxation exercises are useful because you can usually fit them into your day, and they are also helpful to use to keep anxiety and tension under control in problem situations. With practice, you should be able to relax in just a few minutes, or even less.

The idea of relaxation exercises dates back to 1938, when Dr E. Jacobson introduced progressive relaxation, which is effective even for severe tension. He developed a method which demonstrated that if a muscle is first tensed, it will then automatically relax. His patients would progressively tense then relax each muscle group in turn, until the whole body was relaxed and tension reduced. Regular practice was required to acquire the skill. This is the technique of total or deep relaxation. Here are the instructions for this. Give it a try. But first see the box on page 71 for an important warning.

Take care!

Remember that the techniques given in this chapter will help you to relax, but they may also reduce your alertness and may even make you feel drowsy. So while you're working on these, and for around ten minutes afterwards, you shouldn't be looking after anyone, driving, or operating machinery, and you shouldn't stand up suddenly.

Muscles: tense then relax

Now it's time to try out tensing and relaxing your muscles, to help your body to relax. What you will be doing here is not at all strenuous, but does involve tensing your muscles. Read it through first and if you are in any doubt about your physical fitness to try this, check with your doctor. If you have raised blood pressure, it is probably better not to try this activity. There are others later in the chapter which will suit you better.

Exercise: Total relaxation
Lie or sit comfortably, head supported if possible.
   Deliberately make a fist and tense up both hands really hard for five or six seconds . . . . . hold it . . . . . now let the tension go.
   Slowly repeat this for each of the following parts of your body in turn:

Arms
Shoulders
Neck and head
Face
Back and chest
Tummy and bottom
Legs, feet and toes

Relax for a few moments/minutes.
Rouse yourself gradually.

It's worth being aware that a small minority of people may actually feel a bit more tense for the first few moments when trying out a

71

technique involving relaxation or breathing exercises. Regular practice should sort out this difficulty fairly quickly, so don't be put off if it happens to you.

Breathing

Breathing is so important too. Normal breathing is mainly abdominal with little effort being contributed by the muscles of the chest. It is even, quiet and unobtrusive. Just watch a cat or dog lying asleep. It will breathe with its tummy muscles, not its chest. You should breathe like that at rest, but when you are tense your breathing changes. You begin to breathe just a little faster, hardly noticeable. And as part of this 'over-breathing', you use your upper chest more. This can sometimes be quite noticeable if you put one hand on your chest and one on your tummy, and just watch.

The outcome of this change in your breathing is of great significance. You will breathe out too much carbon dioxide leaving your body's delicate chemical balance disturbed. You can easily develop this over-breathing habit and it will affect all parts of your body and all of your body systems, making you feel tired, and unwell. Over-breathing can also fill up your lungs, making you feel as if you can't take a breath, which is a very scary way to feel. In fact if you feel like you can't get a breath, rather than desperately trying to take a breath, what you need to do is to breathe out completely first, then you'll be able to breathe in, as you've created some space!

Breathing is essential for life and is one of the body's sources of fuel. So if we get that very basic of activities wrong, this can upset your whole body chemistry and produce many unusual and unexpected symptoms which you find yourself worrying about. As we've seen, this just makes you more tense. So let's make a start on putting that right.

When we are sleeping, we automatically breathe correctly, and mainly with our tummy or abdomen. So, if you can use the type of breathing experienced in sleep, this can have a very calming effect. This can be so effective, it can even be used instead of other more physical relaxation exercises.

Exercise: Sleep-style breathing

Have a shot at this type of breathing – remember to watch a sleeping cat or dog and you'll see its tummy rising and falling whilst its chest remains still. That's what you're aiming for!

1 Lie or sit with good support.
2 Put one hand flat on your navel, the other on your upper chest.
3 Let your breath go, then breathe in very gently – letting your tummy rise under your hand.
4 In your own time, breathe out again gently, and let your tummy empty and fall again.
5 Continue this gentle breathing, trying to have as little movement of your upper chest as you can.
6 With practice you will manage to breathe in this way without using your hands, and also when you are standing up.

Exercise: Alert-style breathing

But what if you don't want such a calming effect as this? There are many other breathing exercises which will help you to establish normal breathing patterns with a less calming effect. These can be used when you want to be relaxed, but alert at the same time.

So let's try out some of these breathing techniques, which you can use anytime. Many people find such techniques can be a lifeline, as they are so quick and easy to do when needed during a tension-filled day. See which work best for you. Then practise these for a minute or two each day, until you can use them whenever you need them to help you to relax and cope better. All can be done unseen whenever you need to relax. You can do this every so often throughout the day, or whilst waiting in a queue, in a lift, on an escalator, stopped at traffic lights, or during any break-time.

1 Scanning

(a) Breathe in while silently scanning your body for any tension.
(b) As you breathe out, relax any tension you found.
(c) Repeat (a) and (b) several times.

2 Countdown

(a) Focus on your breathing.
(b) Count silently backwards from 10 to 0, saying the next number silently to yourself, each time you breathe out.

3 String Puppet

(a) Let your breath go, then take in a deep breath, hold it for a second or two, then let it go with a sigh of relief, dropping your shoulders and slumping your whole body like a puppet whose strings have been cut.

(b) Repeat (a) (once only).

4 1–2–3 Breathing

(a) Lie or sit with good support.
(b) Let your breath go, then take a gentle breath in to your own slow silent count of 1 . . . . . . 2 . . . . . . 3, then breathe out again in your own time to your own slow and silent count of 1 . . . . . . 2 . . . . . . 3.
(c) Continue gently breathing to this rhythm for a minute or two.

I hope you found trying out these techniques useful. They are simple and straightforward, and very popular with thousands of people. Repeating a simple technique like this for a few moments frequently throughout a day can be very effective in preventing a build-up of tension and over-breathing.

What and how you eat can help

What you eat and what you breathe into your body together provide fuel for your body. They are what give you life and energy, and keep you in balance. So get those right, and you're well on the way to improving how you cope with life's ups and downs. You should have your breathing well on the way to being sorted out already, but what about the other important fuel? What are you eating each day? We've already talked about this in connection with mood swings in Chapter 6. Here again are some useful tips.

- Eat a healthy well-balanced diet.
- Eat a good breakfast.
- Don't skip lunch.
- Avoid sugary snacks or long gaps (2–3 hours at most) without eating – this ensures a constant blood sugar level, which helps to protect you from tension, anger, frustration and aggression.
- Don't drink too much coffee or other drink containing caffeine (e.g. cola).

Exercise can make such a difference

Not only is this generally good for you, and good for elevating your mood as we've seen in Chapter 6, but physical activity has an excellent releasing effect on tension. Some forms of exercise can even allow you to use up feelings of anger and frustration safely and usefully. The key is to find a regular exercise or activity, which you enjoy and which fits in with your lifestyle. You should of course always check with your doctor if you're unsure about your fitness to begin or resume any exercise or activity routine – though walking is generally OK for most people.

How to sleep better

As we've already seen in Chapter 1, being sensitive can make getting to sleep and staying asleep all night difficult. But getting enough quality sleep is vitally important to refresh your body and brain. Here are some useful tips for getting a refreshing night's sleep:

- make sure you take regular exercise during the day, but not just before bed;
- any form of relaxation or breathing exercise will help you get off into a refreshing and restful sleep, or fall back into one if you wake up during the night;
- an over-active mind can be calmed with the methods given in the next chapter;
- make sure your bedroom and your bed aren't too warm – the Better Sleep Council suggests that between 60 and 65°F (15° and 18°C) is best;
- too much light early in the morning in the spring and summer can wake you up too early, so use heavy curtains or blinds that block out the light till you want to wake up;
- a bath a couple of hours before bed helps you to sleep, but don't shower or bath just before bed, as this wakes you up;
- try to keep to the same routine, going to bed and waking up at the same time, even at weekends;
- don't have a heavy meal or tea, coffee or alcohol just before bed.

One change at a time

As mentioned already in previous chapters, attempting only one lifestyle change at a time makes success much more likely. Imagine someone who is already tense trying to reduce their coffee and alcohol consumption the same week as taking up swimming and beginning to eat breakfast! As we've said before, it might be managed the first week perhaps, but what about the following week, and the one after that?

What about your mind?

This chapter has covered lots of practical hints and tips to help you to release the physical tension that being sensitive can mean. Be assured that any effort you put into this will be amply rewarded. But so often, the main difficulty is the constant buzz of activity in your brain, as you chew over and think and re-think the events of the day. The next chapter will help you to calm down this over-active thinking, and give you lots of ideas on how you can begin to relax and refresh your tired and busy mind.

9

Calming your sensitivity 2: mental tips

So far we've focused on relaxing your body. But as you will probably agree, sometimes the main problem is relaxing the mind. Too much thinking, circling around and around in your head, and getting nowhere. Being able to relax physically is an important first step in sorting out this thinking, and will go some way to helping your mind to relax. But sometimes a bit more help is needed.

Brain waves

It helps if you know a bit more about how your brain works, as all this 'calming the mind' can otherwise seem a bit vague. Electrical activity is going on in our brains all the time. This is very low-voltage activity of course, nothing like the strength of the electrical supply we use every day. The reason this activity is called waves is because it is a bit like waves on the sea, some being shallower and faster, and some being deep and slow.

Wave name	Number every second (approx.)	Associated with
Delta	1–4	Deep sleep.
Theta	5–7	Just falling asleep.
Alpha	8–14	Relaxed but alert. Not working on any task in particular. Pleasant and relaxed feelings.
Beta	15–35	Very alert, concentrating on a demanding task. Common during anxiety or panic attacks.

What you are aiming for in relaxing your mind is to encourage it to move from producing mainly Beta waves to producing mainly Alpha waves. You want to be relaxed, but still alert. This is similar to meditation, and is more easily achieved with your eyes closed. If your eyes are open, watching a scene such as waves lapping quietly on the seashore, or a beautiful landscape such as hills, lakes or mountains can be helpful. You can of course use a picture, or a video or computer programme to simulate these for you.

If you are finding it difficult to get to sleep, what you really need to do is to aim first for Alpha waves. This will help you to wind slowly down from the Beta waves which are keeping you awake, through Alpha, and then if you continue relaxing, into Theta, and then into the welcome Delta waves of deep and refreshing sleep. Trying to move straight from Beta to Delta is too much to ask any brain to manage.

Relaxing the mind

The key point in relaxing the mind is to be aware that simply telling yourself not to think about something, or trying to take your mind off your worries, won't achieve a thing. The more you do this, the more you are paying attention to and concentrating on your worries, which in turn can make them worse. This simply encourages Beta waves, which keep you stimulated, and are also required for you to feel anxious or worried. Sometimes your problems can assume even greater proportions and seem much larger than they really are, simply because you keep concentrating on them so much.

To take your mind off your worries, give it something else to think about. And to make it relax, give it something relaxing to think about. Have a look at the suggestions below, try them out, and see what works best for you. Everyone is different and will find some work better than others. Also, it's a new skill, and like physical relaxation needs a bit of practice. But it's well worth it!

The best way to practise relaxing your mind is when you are alone. For most people, time alone is difficult to find. Just taking a bit of time for yourself can make you feel guilty. But, guilt or no guilt, it is so important to ease the tensions in your mind, just as it to ease the strains in your body. You'll be all the happier, healthier and better for it, and everyone around you will notice it and benefit from it. So, no guilt allowed. Here are some suggestions on how to get quality 'me-time':

- get up earlier or go to bed a little bit later than everyone else;
- aim to get home before everyone else so you can have the house to yourself for a while;
- park the car (safely) somewhere on your own;
- in the toilet – at work or elsewhere;
- go for a walk (safely);
- explain to those you live with how important it is for you.

If getting time alone is very difficult, or simply out of the question, the next best thing is to use situations when other people are around you, but are not likely to talk to you or disturb you. We all have these little oases in our day. We just don't capitalize on them enough. Here are some suggestions:

- local library;
- large bookshops – the ones with comfy chairs and coffee;
- when travelling, if you travel alone;
- in the queue at the supermarket, or for the bus;
- wandering round the shops at a quiet time;
- in the sauna;
- gardening;
- in the lift;
- walking up the stairs or on the escalator;
- use a specially designed computer programme;
- play music which you find relaxes you.

As with the previous chapter, do remember not to try any of the following techniques when you need to be fully aware and concentrating on something or someone else. Once you have a quiet place, and you're not going to be disturbed, first use whatever method you have found works best for you to relax your body in the previous chapter. Now try out these methods, for a few minutes each, and see what works best for you.

Exercise: Focus 1

Close your eyes and picture in your mind as clearly and in as much detail as you can a calming scene such as:

- waves lapping on the sea-shore;
- branches blowing in the breeze;
- boats bobbing in the harbour;

- corn swaying in the breeze;
- dark deep green velvet.

Note here which of this list worked best for you: _____

Exercise: Focus 2

Focus your mind absolutely on one of these:

- a calming poem
- prayer
- well-loved face
- well-loved picture

Note here which of this list worked best for you: _____

Exercise: Focus 3

Repeat silently and very slowly a word or phrase such as:

> r ... e ... l ... a ... x ...
> p ... e ... a ... c ... e ...
> peaceful ... and ... calm ...
> let tranquillity ease my mind ...
> so ... ... hum ... ...
> om ... namah ... shivaya ... (sounded 'om numaa shivaa-yuh'
> and means 'I honour my own inner state' in Sanskrit)
> other words which you find calming ...

Note here which of this list worked best for you: _____

Exercise: Imagine

First, relax your body as much as possible, close your eyes, and try imagining yourself in one of the following settings in as much detail and as vividly as you can:

- by the ocean as the waves roll in ... and ... out, ... in ... and ... out, feel the spray, hear the sounds, smell the salt in the air ...
- relaxing on a fluffy cloud, drifting along and warmed by a shining sun ...
- on a grassy mountaintop, tropical forest beneath, the morning rains just over, and warmed by the tropical sun ...
- by a gurgling stream on a warm summer's morning ... hear the birds singing in the trees and feel the grass beneath your feet ...

Note here which of this list worked best for you: _____

*　　*　　*

How did you get on? Everyone will find they have different preferences. Creative people often find it much easier to imagine scenes or pictures. Words and phrases can be easier for most people. Was this true for you? Remember practice is often required to become good at this, but it can be very helpful in managing stress.

Sometimes sensitive people have completely forgotten how to relax both their body and their mind, and they have to re-learn it gradually. What's important is that you try different methods to come up with something which suits you, and then practise the skill until you become good at it, a bit like learning to play the piano or learning to drive, as I mentioned in the previous chapter.

This all may seem like a huge effort, but it really will pay you back life-long dividends, if you can just find the energy now to invest in your future well-being and peace of mind. Put in the work now, and it will all become second nature soon.

When you've chosen which method or methods work best for you, you can add this on to the end of whichever type of physical relaxation technique you found works best, and then practise these every day if you can manage it. You can also use the technique any time you feel the need to relax your mind. When you're trying to get off to sleep, or when you wake in the night and can't get back to sleep for all the worries parading through your mind, these are especially helpful times to use these new skills.

Importance of social support

It has been shown that people who don't have much social support in their lives are vulnerable to tension and stress. Without friends, family or a partner to talk to, they may find it difficult to cope with the daily hassles and stresses of life. And if you are alone a lot, you may find that these prey on your mind more than most.

But lonely people are not the only people who might lack social support. Anyone living in a family or a neighbourhood which does not provide this support is also vulnerable. You can live with many other people, and still feel completely alone. Aim to take action if your existing support system could do with some building up – for example, if you have a partner, colleague or family member who is openly critical and unsupportive, or you have a friend who keeps telling you to pull yourself together, or that you're too sensitive for your own good, or gives other unhelpful advice.

All of us need positive support in our lives. This makes today's problematic life easier to cope with and cushions its impact. Have a think about those people who might be supportive to you, and how you could best encourage and make better use of that support. It's not weak to need or look for support – it's positively good for our health. Having someone who cares about us, and who is interested in what we do, can bring both a relief of existing problems and worries, but it can also prevent us feeling tense and nervous in the first place. A problem shared with the right person really is a problem halved. But that person must be someone you can trust.

This important support can come from four places:

1 your family and/or friends
2 your partner (if you have one)
3 your local community
4 at work

SOCIAL SUPPORT QUESTIONNAIRE

Have a think about those around you and the community you live in.

- Do you have a partner?   YES/NO

If YES

- Is your partner supportive?   YES/NO

If YES

- How does your partner show this to you?

- Do you have members of your family
  who are or could be supportive?   YES/NO

If YES

- List their names here:

- Do you have friends who could be supportive?   YES/NO

If YES

- List their names here:

- What about at work – is there some kind of support available there?

- What kind of support do you feel that you need the most?

- How do you think you could go about getting this support?

If you are lucky enough to have a good support system already, make maximum use of it, as an outlet for feelings and as a source of encouragement. You should also accept offers of help, and delegate to others to relieve pressure. No need to feel guilty for doing this. But if your existing support system could do with some building up, or if you're starting at the beginning and trying to build one for yourself, here are some suggestions – tick those you could try:

☐ Take it one step at a time.

☐ Encourage and maintain your existing supportive relationships.

☐ If someone important doesn't understand, if you think it would help, let them read some of this book to help them to understand better, or try explaining it yourself.

☐ Create new supportive relationships.

☐ Get more involved in your community.

☐ Seek support from an appropriate community organization.

☐ Join a local social club or other group.

☐ Consult local directories, libraries, or advice centres for suitable support, leisure or social facilities.

☐ Think about using any support facilities which are offered at work.

☐ There are numerous confidential support and counselling groups in every community. Seeking help from these or anywhere else is in no way a sign of weakness. It is indeed a strength to recognize that sometimes, someone else perhaps has some of the answers.

10

When sensitivity gets out of hand

Managed carefully, sensitivity, hand in hand with a host of positive characteristics such as empathy and intuition, can make for a caring and successful life. But sometimes, with the best will in the world, sensitivity can get out of hand, and cause acute and disabling problems. The result is that you may not fulfil your potential, be it in your personal or professional life.

As we've already established, as a sensitive person you may be more likely to suffer from tension, anxiety and stress, because of how you react to everyday life. When we are tense and stressed, the automatic part of our nervous system, the part which keeps us breathing and our heart beating automatically, without us having to think about it, becomes highly aroused.

This increased arousal is a necessary part of our biological make-up, and evolved in our caveman ancestors as a self-preservation mechanism, to prepare them to cope *physically* with whatever dangerous situations they might experience. We breathe faster, think faster, our heart beats faster, our muscles become taut and ready for action, our blood sugar levels rise to give us an energy boost, increased amounts of adrenalin are produced, and so on. All this physiological activity is to prepare us for instant and effective action. In the case of an approaching snarling sabre-toothed tiger, this instant automatic arousal prepared the cave men to either 'fight' the animal or 'flee' as fast as they could. This all happened automatically, because if our ancestors had taken time to think about it, it would have been too late.

In terms of human evolution, this development has occurred relatively recently, therefore our bodies still react to stress in exactly the same way today. However, in our modern world, stress is unlikely to arise from *physically* dangerous situations. More likely sources of stress would be our manager, a quarrelsome neighbour, or another bill coming through the letterbox. But we can't fight our line manager, or run away from our neighbour or our debts, much as we might want to. In today's world there is seldom a *physical* outlet for the ancient 'fight or flight' reaction, and the arousal it produces. All those major bodily changes have no outlet, leaving you feeling very uneasy.

Stress

It is important to remember that if you do learn to manage your tension and stress at a physiological level, by whatever way you find to be effective, then the more serious results of stress will also be controlled. Manage your immediate stress reactions, and you manage the results of your stress. Previous chapters, especially Chapters 8 and 9, have outlined ways of doing this and Chapter 11 will give you still more guidance on this. But what are the possible outcomes if you aren't able to control your stress reactions? David came to me for advice some years ago; here is his story.

David A.

David is a self-employed painter and decorator, aged 44, married with two teenage sons. He likes to work on his own as he believes he just doesn't get on well working with other people. When working with other people he found that they always seemed to find fault with his work, or would make suggestions for changes in the business, or bring in new ways of doing things, and so he kept having arguments with them. Business used to be really good, but has been slowly declining of late, as he hasn't kept up with the modern trends. He just can't see how he is going to maintain the standard of living to which his family has become accustomed, for much longer. This has been constantly on his mind for months, and he feels physically tense and tired a lot of the time. Three days ago, without any warning, he suddenly had a panic attack whilst at work, and was so terrified by it that he went straight home excusing himself by saying he suddenly felt sick. He actually thought he was going mad, and was scared to tell his wife, or anybody else. He had two days in bed, explaining it away with a stomach upset. During the two days in bed, he was so terrified of having another of these dreadful attacks that his fear of going out of the house grew. The next day, when he tried to go back to work, he couldn't even make it out of the front door, because of shaking, palpitations and a feeling of acute fear and panic. His wife called an ambulance, fearing he was having a heart attack.

Panic attacks

A panic attack like David's is a very common outcome of long-term tension and stress. Your stomach may churn, heart race, your breathing may be rapid, you may sweat, feel faint, feel overwhelming fear and panic, and have a sense of impending disaster, along with a pressing need to escape from the situation you find yourself in. Clearly this is a very distressing and frightening way to feel.

Panic attacks like this are a form of acute anxiety, and are the body's normal reaction to *physical* danger. In fact the human species couldn't have survived this long without it.

Though this reaction developed as a primitive response to physical danger, such as the infamous sabre-toothed tiger, it is just as easily brought into play in today's high-speed world by psychological danger. In other words, when there is danger to us as a person, for example when we fear losing face, or not being able to cope, or being embarrassed in public, or if we feel our lives are out of control. Our brain can't really tell the difference. I first met Kirsty about five years ago when she was experiencing severe but confusing symptoms.

Kirsty C.
Kirsty walked into my consulting room, her face a mixture of fear and worry. She was 32, and worked full-time. Her eyes were downcast and she trembled as she slowly and hesitantly explained to me that she was sure she was going mad. Yesterday at work she had 'come over all peculiar'. She couldn't think straight, was convinced something terrible was about to happen, and her heart had pounded. She had also had a feeling of acute panic, and had found herself rushing out of the office without explaining. The funny thing was that as soon as she got home, she felt fine again. What was happening to her? Was this a nervous breakdown? What would everyone think? What if it should happen again? Gentle questioning revealed that she had been under pressure for some weeks as she was moving house, and had already bought a house, but couldn't sell her own. She had split up with yet another boyfriend, as she never seemed to be able to keep a relationship going. She wasn't sleeping well, and felt tired all the time.

Kirsty wasn't really aware that what she was experiencing was a form of panic. A panic attack feels like being the victim of a terrifying attack over which you appear to have absolutely no control. You are more likely to have this feeling of a lack of control if you have an 'external locus of control' which we discussed in Chapter 5. You can be convinced you are going mad or are about to die.

If you don't regain control over these attacks, which seem to strike out of the blue, a vicious circle can quickly, if not immediately, establish itself. Still higher levels of arousal and stress will be produced as you worry about the next attack, and you will implement avoidance behaviour for situations which you fear may provoke another attack. It won't occur to you that *you* can do something about it *yourself*. The fleeting thought, 'What if I panic now?' can immediately set off that feared and dreaded attack. What can be done if you have panic attacks?

How to cope with a panic attack – The 'Pause' routine

If you have experienced a panic attack, think about the first signs of the attack. This might have been a lurch in the stomach, a thought that flashed across your mind, your heart rate rising, or anything else you've noticed. Be on the look out for these initial signs, and when you notice them, you should immediately take the following steps:

Pause . . . and make yourself comfortable (sit down, lean on something, etc.),
Absorb . . . details of your environment and what's going on around you,
Use . . . any method of relaxing quickly which works for you, then
Slowly . . . when you feel better,
Ease . . . yourself back into what you were doing.

So this is where all that practising with quick ways of relaxing from Chapter 8 pays off. When using the PAUSE routine, you can use whichever method of relaxing has worked best for you – be it any of the types of relaxation or breathing techniques you read about earlier.

If you have panic attacks, the key is to catch them early, and stop them in their tracks. This puts you firmly back in control. Simply telling yourself not to panic will have absolutely no effect. This primitive reaction won't react to you telling it what to do, you have to react physically to slow down and stop another physical reaction.

Don't be put off if this method doesn't work the first or even second time you try it. It takes a bit of practice, and a bit of determination, but once you get it, you'll never forget it, and it is very effective.

Tension can lead to other conditions

As we've seen, prolonged tension can lead to panic attacks and anxiety. And these can very quickly lead to people avoiding situations in which they fear they may panic. Unfortunately, avoidance can easily develop into a phobia, which is more common than you might think. One review estimated that 13 per cent of us will have a problem with panic attacks and phobias in our lifetime. That's several people on an average street. Common though it is, it's not something people tend to talk about.

The phobias that are most likely to develop due to sensitivity getting out of hand are agoraphobia, and social phobia. And contrary to popular belief, these phobias are in no way irrational. In most cases, it is not an illogical fear that lies at the heart of these phobias, but the fear of suffering a panic attack or some other symptoms in public. People are not actually afraid of going outside, or socializing with their friends; they fear these unpleasant symptoms, or being embarrassed in public. For the sufferer there is no logical explanation for the panic attack, so the initial often terrifying attack quickly becomes associated with where it happened, leading to ever more extreme avoidance behaviour, and further anxiety. The unconscious conclusion is that if no other explanation for the panic attack is forthcoming, the person who suffers the attack concludes that it must have been something to do with where they were and what they were doing at the time. Alternatively, and this is often the case, the person decides that they must be going mad. But they aren't of course; it's just a normal behaviour, which has got out of hand.

Agoraphobia

An often underestimated and misunderstood condition, agoraphobia affects significantly more women than men, though the reasons for this are not yet clear. This may simply be because women are more likely to admit to it, or perhaps they are more likely to have a home-based lifestyle, which fosters the development of agoraphobia. Often mistaken to mean the fear of open spaces, agoraphobia is in fact a fear of leaving the security of home, particularly if required to go to crowded places, or to wait in a queue of any kind. Again it is the symptoms experienced when outside which are feared, not being outside in itself. Unpleasant symptoms experienced when out of the home become associated with being away from home, and a pattern of avoidance and increased fear can very easily spiral out of control.

It is not uncommon for professional and business men or women to suffer from agoraphobia, yet still manage to function completely adequately, so long as they are able to travel around by car. For agoraphobics, the car is often a substitute for the security of the home, and they simply take it with them, wherever they go, like a security blanket. A friend, partner, relative or colleague can fill the same role.

Social phobia

Again more common than perhaps assumed, social phobia can develop in a similar way to agoraphobia. The main difference is probably that the situation avoided is that of having to 'perform' in some way in front of one or more people. Having to have a conversation, dance, sign a document, give a talk or demonstration, eat or drink, may all become a source of embarrassment or fear if visible symptoms of tension and stress occur. Blushing, sweating, shaking, panicking, stammering, feeling off balance or light-headed, can all be caused by stress, and all can encourage avoidance of a range of social situations. The acid test of whether a social phobia is involved is whether the person can perform the required behaviour when alone, and only succumbs to anxiety when other people are present. When Gary came to see me, he was very distressed because of the problems caused by embarrassment.

Gary J.

Gary is 26 and had just had an appraisal at work before going out at lunchtime to go to the bank. The appraisal hadn't gone well, and he was feeling upset and hurt at what had been said to him. When he was signing a form at the bank that lunchtime, he found his hand shook a little. He felt very embarrassed, and couldn't understand why this had happened. Then a week or two later, his hand shook when he was having a drink with his friends, so now he avoids outings with his friends in case it happens again and they laugh at him. He is now so scared of his hand shaking that his fear has made it happen more often, reinforcing the belief that it will happen. He feels that he is going to pieces, and now won't go out anywhere that his shaking hand may be seen by others. He has even begun to avoid eating with his family in case his hand shakes when eating his meal.

Obsessive compulsive disorder (OCD)

There are numerous obsessions and compulsions that are quite harmless. Many people simply have to put a pinch of salt over their left shoulder after spilling any salt, will not walk on the lines of the pavement or under a ladder, must have ornaments or books displayed in a certain way, or find themselves checking twice that the gas is off or the door locked, even though they know they've just checked it. If these various needs are not met, such people suffer a slight pang of anxiety. Giving in and performing the behaviour will reduce that anxiety. This is the kind of behaviour on which obsessive compulsive disorder (OCD) can gradually be built, if it is taken to extremes.

If you are tense and anxious, it's relatively easy to slip into unusual habits which can reduce your anxiety and make you feel better, even temporarily. You might develop checking rituals, or little phrases you have to say at certain times, or find you wash your hands or tidy the house too thoroughly and too often. This, again, is normal behaviour taken to extremes. Many OCD sufferers never seek help because of the embarrassment or because of the constraints of the condition, but recent studies suggest it to be more common than previously thought. There are likely to be around 100 people with a disabling phobia or OCD in the average GP's list of 2,000 patients. Linda is one example.

Linda G.
Linda is 32, and works part-time in a specialist sweet shop near to her home to help make ends meet, as her husband has a very low-paid job. She finds life a strain, as she is always arguing with Pete, her husband, who says she's too sensitive for her own good. She also finds she can't keep friends easily, and is always upset with one of the neighbours about something. One day a few months ago, she checked the cooker was off as usual before leaving for work, but as soon as she had locked the front door, she felt anxious in case the gas hob was still on even though she had just checked it. Might as well make sure, she thought, better safe than sorry. So she returned to check. The next day she found herself doing the same thing, checking twice, as she felt anxious if she didn't make sure, and there was no harm in checking. This went on for a few weeks, until one day she found herself having to check three times in order to be convinced the gas really was off, and to reduce her anxiety. Sometimes she would get halfway to work, then have to come back to check. Now after several months, she has to allow an extra ten minutes to get ready for work, as she can't relax unless she checks four times that the gas is off before leaving. She knows this is stupid, but she just can't

help herself. The anxiety gets so bad if she tries not to do it that she just can't bear it. She's scared to tell anyone in case they think she's going mad.

Obsessions are intrusive unwanted thoughts, ideas or impulses, which repeatedly recur in a person's mind, usually of a frightening or repulsive nature. Compulsions, sometimes known as rituals, are behaviours repeated to reduce the anxiety caused by the obsessive thought. Linda's obsessive thought, for example, was of the house blowing up due to a gas explosion, and her compulsion was to check the gas was off. Likewise if a person has obsessive thoughts centred on a fear of dirt or germs, then they may compulsively wash and clean themselves and the house to reduce the anxiety caused by the thoughts. Other common obsessive thoughts include repetitive counting, blasphemous thoughts, or vivid images of harming or even killing a loved family member. The compulsions most commonly reported include excessive hand-washing, house-cleaning, and the repeated checking of water, gas or electricity.

Post-traumatic stress disorder (PTSD)

If you are highly sensitive and you are unlucky enough to be involved in a serious accident, crime or other traumatic event, you may well be more affected by your experiences than others. PTSD has come very much into the public eye in recent years, in the wake of many disasters and war experiences, and is a condition which can follow an experience which is out of the range of everyday human experience. Even jurors in particularly traumatic court cases can be affected, simply by hearing about a traumatic event, and seeing pictures of it.

You may be surprised to find that the degree of trauma experienced by an individual is not fixed by the gravity of the event itself, but by how strongly the person reacts to it. There may even be a delay in the development of the disorder, with symptoms not occurring for months or even years after the event.

This condition requires treatment from a psychiatrist or clinical psychologist, and is dealt with differently from general stress. If you are in any way concerned you should have a talk with your GP. Here are the three main signs of PTSD:

1 re-experiencing the event through nightmares, flashbacks, hallucinations, or intense reaction to similar events or anniversaries of the event;
2 avoidance of anything linked to the trauma, poor memory of it or general numbing of emotions;
3 increased arousal of the nervous system shown by difficulty falling or staying asleep, outbursts of anger, or an excessive startle response.

What help is available?

There is much that can be done if you recognize yourself in any of the descriptions given in this chapter. Your GP should be your first port of call, and you could then be referred to a specialist who will most likely use techniques such as progressive desensitization to treat you. This treatment, sometimes called Cognitive Behaviour Therapy or CBT, enables you to gradually relearn normal behaviour and thinking patterns.

For phobias this involves a process of approaching the feared situation one step at a time over a period of time. The agoraphobic person might begin by simply standing in the doorway; once that is mastered through frequent practice, they will then progress to the end of the path, and so on. For OCD, the patient will gradually cut down on the compulsive behaviour. Instead of checking the gas is off six times, they will practise checking only five times. In either case, relaxation and breathing exercises are used to reduce the feelings of anxiety provoked by these small steps towards everyday behaviour. Medication can also make a huge difference in most cases.

Should you experience any of these conditions, effective treatment is available. You shouldn't have to suffer in silence. Your doctor will understand, and will be able to help you.

11

How to make your thinking style work better for you

I'm sure that you'll be wondering what your thinking has to do with being sensitive. Surely thinking is just an automatic function, an innate part of who you are that can't be changed. How can it have the least effect on your life? And what is a thinking style anyway?

The over-sensitive person may have an especially active imagination, who 'sees' disasters such as plane crashes in gory detail, and can forecast the future so vividly that events yet to come already seem real and threatening. As a particularly sensitive person you may be more perceptive, especially of subtle matters that others would miss, and you may also be more analytic than most. All these factors can mean that your way of thinking almost predisposes you to worrying a lot about things which may or may not happen, thereby making you tense and anxious a substantial part of the time. Instead of thinking it'll never happen to me, you're more inclined to be thinking, of course that can happen to me, the only question is when?

Do you recognize yourself in any of these descriptions? If so, I'm not trying to suggest that you have any kind of psychological problem, I simply want to highlight that there are many ways of thinking which are unhelpful in today's world.

Anybody can find themselves engaged in this kind of thought process. This chapter will explain this, and give you ideas on how you can change and adapt your thinking to be more constructive. Your thinking style is just a combination of habits you've acquired over your lifetime, much of it in childhood, and much of it by unconsciously copying those around you. Parents, teachers, friends, siblings, and wider family can all have affected how you think. You don't just learn the good stuff from your parents, you can easily pick up bad habits too. It's nobody's fault, that's just life. Your parents will have picked up their habits from their parents too. But there is much you can do to change these unconstructive thinking patterns.

Thinking habits

We all know people who remain positive and unbowed in the face of difficult circumstances, and others who simply crumple and give up hope. The difference lies entirely in how these individuals think about their situation. Is the glass half full or half empty? The difference is in their attitude to life – how they think about it. Most of us fit in somewhere between these two extremes. Where do you think you might fit in?

Changing how we think about the world may not in itself be enough to deal with particularly extreme situations, for example coping with bereavement or an abusive relationship, but in the greyer areas of life, our appraisal or judgement of the situation can have a major impact on whether we experience tension and anxiety or not. How we think about the world can even be a significant cause of tension in itself.

How we think can affect us in two distinct ways:

1 It determines our reaction to a difficult situation i.e. being crushed by it, or taking it in our stride, or somewhere in between. Being sensitive is not just about the situations we find ourselves in – it's about our *attitude* towards those situations.
2 It can actually be the *cause of the feeling of being sensitive in the first place*, e.g. expecting too much of ourselves, expecting too much of other people.

Of course, in a complex world, both of these results can intertwine and determine whether we perceive our everyday lives as being filled with tension and distress or not.

Since the 1960s there have been many developments on the topic of how everyday patterns of thought and belief can encourage and exacerbate our tendency to be sensitive and to feel tense. This has given us wide-ranging approaches to how you can alter your thinking to make you less sensitive. The overarching link in these various approaches is to become aware of the thinking styles and beliefs which may be causing problems, and then to take on board suggestions as to how these might be changed. For many people, simply becoming aware of your established patterns of thought along with their effects can be enough to effect a substantial, effective and long-lasting change. To anyone not familiar with such ideas, they may seem unusual, strange even, but you become familiar with the ideas very quickly. Most people find the following concepts fascinating, enlightening and even liberating. They also find these techniques surprisingly effective.

Unhelpful thinking

Aaron Beck is a well-known name in the study of how we think, and how this can affect our behaviour. He explains that there are many, many ways in which we think that are unhelpful. Anyone can fall victim to these, but if you are sensitive, it is likely that you use several or more of the following habits in your everyday thinking. Read them and see if you recognize yourself in any of them:

Negative thinking

Overlooking the positive side of each day or situation because for some reason, it doesn't count. You dwell on and react to only the negative side of things, and can let one negative aspect of an otherwise good day colour your whole reaction. Why doesn't the positive side count just as much, if not more? See later in this chapter for more about positive thinking.

Black and white thinking

Seeing everything in black and white instead of shades of grey as most things really are. You might see people as either good or bad with nothing at all in between, or yourself or your life as either a total success or a total failure. Tell yourself now – life is in shades of grey, there's no such thing as black and white – most people and most people's lives are somewhere between the two.

Jumping to conclusions

Making decisions or making assumptions about a situation without weighing up the evidence for and against. For example, deciding that your new neighbours don't like you because they couldn't come for a drink when you invited them. If you believe this rather than the more obvious reason – that they really had something else on that night – then you are jumping to conclusions and you need to challenge your thoughts more. Ask yourself what you would tell a friend in the same situation. Think about what evidence there really is for what you are thinking. Which is the most likely reason?

Exaggerated thinking

Always assuming the worst possible outcome in situations. For example, if your partner is ten minutes late home, you imagine him or her in a terrible car accident, or having an affair with a colleague.

If someone is slightly off-hand with you, you believe that they are upset with you about some major faux pas. In cases like this ask yourself what the chances are that you are right. What is the most probable explanation? What would you say to a friend worrying about the same thing?

Mind reading

You believe you know what someone else is thinking. And of course the reality is that you have no idea at all. There are absolutely no limits to what people might be thinking about something; how likely is it then that are you going to get it spot on? You don't have all the evidence you need to start drawing any conclusions.

Inappropriate blaming

Blaming yourself for something which, in reality, you had no control over. This happens especially in hindsight. If you hadn't stopped to get a paper, you wouldn't have missed the train and been late, and you would have been there to get your mother to the hospital more quickly when she had a stroke. Ask yourself in cases like this: how were you to know? What would you say to a friend that this had happened to? What other factors led to the stroke? Should her neighbour be blaming herself for not popping in at just the right time? Tell yourself that we can't ever know the consequences of each action and if we thought about all of these every time we did something, we'd never do anything.

Holding unhelpful beliefs

It isn't only how you think which can be unconstructive. Underlying how we think is our belief system, and that too can be unhelpful. In 1962, Dr Albert Ellis explained how tension and anxiety can be the outcome of the beliefs which we hold about the world. He described these as irrational beliefs in the sense that they are inflexible and dogmatic. Not that these irrational beliefs are indicative of a problem or an illness; such beliefs are extremely common and entirely 'normal'.

Here are a few taken from an extensive list of examples, and it is easy to see how holding even one of these beliefs can make life stressful even in the absence of major negative life events.

- Life should be fair.
- I should be able to do everything well.
- There should be a perfect solution for everything.

- I need everyone's approval for everything I do.
- I should not make a mistake.

Most of this thinking is the result of growing up and living in a world where performance standards are set high, praise for a job well done is seen as encouraging an undesirable inflated ego, and criticism of mistakes is never far away. All of this has produced low self-esteem and fear of failure in many people. If someone can become aware of and challenge these beliefs, they should be able to ease the tension and anxiety produced by them.

If you hold such irrational beliefs it is important to understand that they are not based on an undisputed truth, but have their roots in your childhood and the culture around you. Ask yourself where these beliefs are written down or stated. Here is the same set of irrational or mistaken beliefs, along with ways of challenging them.

- Life should be fair. (Who says? How could it possibly be?)
- I should be able to do everything well. (Who says? Do you know anyone else who can?)
- There should be a perfect solution for everything. (Who says? How could there be?)
- I need everyone's approval for everything I do. (Why? Who says? Is it possible anyway? You can't please all the people all the time.)
- I should not make a mistake. (Do you know anyone who doesn't make lots of them?)

Many common tension-inducing beliefs include the words 'ought', 'should' or 'must':

- I ought to have done that better.
- I must cope with everything.
- I should have done that better.
- I must not make a mistake.
- I must get all this done today.

If you find that you hold such beliefs you must ask yourself why you believe this to be true, who prescribes this and whether other people adhere to these standards.

Other beliefs and thoughts involve the words 'awful', 'terrible' or 'can't stand it', which usually exaggerate the reality of the situation:

- I can't stand this. (You've stood things like this before, you can do it again. Is it really as bad as all that?)
- This is absolutely awful/terrible. (Some things are, but is this? What words have you left to use if something even worse happens?)

Katy L.
Katy is in a long-term relationship with her partner, Greig. They get on well together, have a comfortable flat, and are thinking of starting a family soon. But Katy feels tense and worried a lot of the time. She can't think of any reason for this.

When I asked her to describe her usual day, she said:

> I have to get up at 6.30 a.m. as I must get the washing into the machine and tidy round the house before I leave for work. Greig really hates it if the house is untidy, and I just hate to upset him. I have to give a lift to Jenny who works with me, and that takes me out of my way, so it takes an hour to get to work. Jenny would be offended if I didn't give her a lift. I ought to do the food shopping in my lunch hour, but I can't always manage that. I have this absolutely awful job at the supermarket. I can't stand it, but we need the money. Then I rush home to cook dinner. I really ought to do more home cooking for Greig, and have his parents and brother round for a meal more often, but trying to fit everything in is so terribly difficult. It isn't fair really, I try so hard, but I never seem to get it right. There must be some easy answer to it all, because everybody else seems to cope better than I do. I really feel that I'm just letting everyone down.

Much of Katy's thinking, rather than the situation itself, is causing her unnecessary tension. She sets rules and expectations for herself which are impossible to meet, exaggerates situations, and is angry with life because it doesn't all work out the way she wants. It is quite common for much of this type of thinking to interlock with a kind of 'ideology of life'.

I am not suggesting that Katy is to blame or that she deliberately thinks in this way. These are thinking habits and irrational beliefs which can creep up on anyone and are very common indeed in today's hectic world where such great emphasis is put on success and coping. Do you recognize anything of yourself in Katy's account of life?

Thinking more positively

Donald Meichenbaum has developed techniques based on the idea that our self-speech, the constant inner dialogue we have with ourselves, exerts considerable control over our behaviour. People may therefore have a very negative and self-defeating style of self-speech, which compounds already low self-esteem. You might find it interesting to jot down some of the thoughts which flit in and out of your head throughout a morning. You may be surprised by what you find.

This negative style of self-speech is another common symptom of modern life, and might include thoughts such as:

- This is going to be really difficult, I don't think I can cope with it.
- I'll never manage this.
- Here we go with another boring day.
- Why do I bother with this?
- This is terrible.
- How awful.
- I'm hopeless at this.
- Oh no, here we go again.

This inner speech is a habit, and it is important to remember that habits can be changed. If you find yourself using such 'negative self-talk', replace it with a more positive version. Here are some examples:

- I've coped with this before, so I can do it again.
- I know I can do this if I try.
- I know I can do this quite well, and that should be good enough.

It's all about reprogramming your automatic thoughts to be more realistic and more positive. It takes a bit of practice, but it really does work. Einstein thought there were two ways to live your life: one, as though nothing were a miracle; the other, as though everything were a miracle.

Gaining a sense of control

Control is a theme which has run through much of the book so far, and we return to it here. We saw how people vary in the extent to which they feel they can affect their situation, and have some control over what happens to them. Those with what was described as an 'external locus of control' feel they have very little control, may be appraising their situation inappropriately and subsequently won't have taken any of the available steps that could reduce their tension.

The objective is to empower such people and give them the means to deal with their difficulties effectively, which is particularly pertinent if you are too sensitive. We have seen that there are many situations over which people really do have little control, but whenever it is possible, people who feel they can do nothing to affect their situation require encouragement to change their mind and take action.

This idea may lie at the heart of the difference between people who crumple and those who flourish when faced with adversity. The former sees the situation as beyond their control and gives up, whilst the latter takes control and puts into place the required action to turn the situation around.

And lastly

The American psychologist and philosopher William James believed that the greatest revolution of our generation was the discovery that human beings, by changing the inner attitudes of their minds, can change the outer aspects of their lives. I do hope you're in the process of discovering this for yourself!

- It could be particularly useful to highlight in this chapter anything which you feel is helpful for you or that you feel applies directly to you. Being aware is half the battle.
- If you haven't already done this, go back and do this now.
- A little bit at a time, try out some of the advice given – but as usual, don't rush at it, a lifetime's habits take time to change.
- Refer back to this chapter every so often to remind yourself of the various ideas. This will also help you monitor how your thinking is changing.

12

The way forward

Now that we are approaching the end of the book, it is a good time to talk about moving forward and implementing any of the changes you've decided you would like to build into your life from now on. I hope that you've picked up lots of new ideas, not only about how to cope better with being highly sensitive, but also about how to utilize its positive side too. You will want to take these ideas on board very gradually over the next days, weeks and months, and make your sensitivity begin to work for you, and not against you.

In this final chapter, I'll help you to make up a 'Big Picture' of the most important points in the book for you. I'll also help you to make up your own 'Personal Action Plan', which will translate these points into concrete steps for you to put into action in the coming weeks and months.

Motivation

No doubt about it, sometimes ongoing lack of confidence can erode motivation – perhaps you may feel tired from years of battling with difficulties as well as the effects of your sensitivities, or feel it's just not worthwhile making the effort to start anything new.

However, the fact that you are reading this book shows you are already motivated and ready for change. And, the fact that you have reached the final chapter, and you're still here with me, says you are still just as enthusiastic and committed to change! I hope that throughout each chapter I have given you even more motivation. Not only that, but I hope I've given you the tools to do the job. Making up your 'Big Picture' and your 'Personal Action Plan' will also help to firm up and formulate your plans, and make it more likely that you will have the necessary motivation and enthusiasm to follow them through. You'll have a road map with your route to the future marked clearly on it.

It is crucial that you don't just *think* about making changes but take action and make the changes. You owe it to yourself to actually put these plans into effect. Don't be saying to yourself, 'I think I'll . . .', or 'Maybe I'll . . .', or worse still, 'When I have the time . . .', or the real action stopper 'This isn't a good time, I'll wait till things are better . . .'

There is never 'a good time' or the 'right time' to make changes in your life for the better. If you wait for the right time, it will never come, and you'll never do anything. The right time is now. And your motto from now on should be:

'*I can, I will, and I'm going to . . .*'

Preparing to do something which might make you anxious

As part of the process of changing, you may decide to try out some new things. Whatever you decide to do that's new to you, there's a chance that this might make you feel a bit tense or anxious at first. This can put you off, and reduce your motivation. With time and practice, these difficulties will disappear. But in the meantime, here are some suggestions, which will help to make tackling new things much easier.

- Become good at relaxing quickly, and without anyone knowing, so that you can use this when you're trying something new. Some suggestions for this were given in Chapters 8 and 9.
- Watch out for 'negative self-talk' in the days or weeks beforehand, such as 'I'm going to make a fool of myself' or 'I'm useless at this.' This builds your anxiety and increases your self-doubt. Replace such self-talk with positive and realistic thoughts such as, 'If I use relaxation I can do this', or, 'I am a capable person and I can manage this' or, 'I've done this before, and I can do it again.' See Chapter 11 for more on this.
- Use 'thought-blocking' when you have negative or anxious thoughts. That is, think 'STOP' and keep repeating this in your mind until your thoughts go on to something else. You can also use any other word or phrase you choose, or an image or idea such as a favourite place, person, animal, flower etc., to block out the worrying thought until your mind wanders elsewhere, as it will. We covered some ideas for this in Chapter 9. You may need many repetitions to start with, to make this work for you, but you soon get better at this. It can be very effective, and prevents tension building.

Visualization can help

It may sound strange, but visualization can have a very powerful and unexpectedly positive effect. It can really affect how you feel about yourself, and also how things go when you try something new. Visualization is in fact a rather straightforward idea.

What to do is, while sitting quietly and relaxed, to build up a picture in your mind's eye of a chosen situation, as vividly and in as much detail as you can: colours, smells, sights, how things feel, sounds, speech and so on. Whenever you feel any tension or anxiety associated with what you are visualizing, you use a quick method of relaxing to reduce that anxiety. When the anxiety falls, you continue with the visualization.

When you do this, it's as if facing up to it all in your mind before actually dealing with a particular event or situation in real life. It takes the sting out of any anxiety you might feel beforehand, by making it feel familiar when the day arrives. On the day, it's as if you've 'been there and done that' many times already, but in a relaxed state of mind, so it produces much less tension.

Beyond this book

If a particular topic I've covered in this book has sparked your interest, or seemed particularly relevant to you, you can follow this up by reading further into the subject (see Useful resources on page 112). You may even want to take a course, or see a life coach, perhaps on subjects like stress management, relaxation, meditation, assertiveness, confidence building and so on (these should be available in your local area). If you want to make inroads into your physical appearance and well-being, there's a gym, beautician and hairdresser on almost every corner these days. Even if money is tight, there are many funded schemes which you can join, and which will help you to become fit, healthy and active. The sky is really the limit these days, if you want it enough.

There are also countless organizations out there with specialist knowledge or advice and support on a wealth of subjects, as well as counsellors ready and able to take things further with you if you feel the need, and much of this is free. The Internet will provide you with an abundance of information, and the British Association for Counselling and Psychotherapy keeps a register of approved counsellors throughout the UK (see Useful resources on page 112).

Take change step by step
Remember, this book is just a starting point. I've given you the means to change your life in many ways, permanently, but you can't do it all overnight. There is much for you to do, and this will all take time. Remember, taking one step at a time is always the surest and best way to

make and maintain steady progress. You can use this book as a reference and a reminder of where you are, and what your next step should be. Nothing is set in a tablet of stone, but you'll have it there to keep you on track, reviewing and adapting as you go along.

Ups and downs

It would be wrong for me to paint a completely rosy picture of constant improvement and progress in coping better with your sensitivity. Just like anything else in life, you may well experience ups and downs over the next weeks and months. You may already have found this out for yourself.

This is no different from learning anything new. One day everything just slots into place, whilst on other days, we're all fingers and thumbs and can't do anything right. But the bad day soon passes, to be replaced by a number of better, more hopeful and more useful days, when we've taken another step forward and have a more positive attitude to life.

Think of anything new you've ever had to learn, and I'm sure you'll agree this is so: driving, keyboard skills, skiing, cooking, golf, swimming, whatever. Don't be put off by the occasional bad day or even a more lengthy setback. These are all part and parcel of the learning process and of life itself.

Summing up and the 'Big Picture'

This book has covered quite a number of issues – what 'sensitivity' is, why people become sensitive, and what its many positive aspects are. We've also looked at how to relax body and mind, and how to think in a more productive, positive and inspirational way. We've also thought about how to deal with moods, confidence and assertiveness, and control in your life. It's probably useful at this stage to try to pull all these loose ends together, so that you can see your own 'bigger picture'. I suggest that now you should flick back through this book, and complete the 'Big Picture' and 'Personal Action Plan' which follow.

The Big Picture

On pages 106–8 there is a template for your Big Picture ready to complete. What you need to do is to thumb back through the entire book, then complete the following as best you can. Take as much time as you need. There is no rush – it can take a bit of time and thoughtful reflection . . .

MY BIG PICTURE

From your reading of Chapter 3, why do you think you are a sensitive person?

What benefits (if any) have you gained from having a better under-standing of why you are sensitive?

What are the main problems you have been having because of your sensitivity? (Check back to Chapter 1 if you need to.)

From your reading of Chapter 2, what for you are the positive aspects of being sensitive? List as many as you can here:

List here 7 or 8 positive things you've learned about yourself by reading this book (check back to Chapter 4 if you need to):

What things do you think you can do to become more confident? (Check back to Chapter 4 if you need to.)

If you have problems with moods or mood swings, what are the main ways you can cope better with these? (Check back to Chapter 6 if you need to.)

If you want to become more assertive, what are the main ways you could do this? (Check back to Chapter 7 if you need to.)

If you want to become more relaxed, what are the main ways you could do this? (Check back to Chapters 8 and 9 if you need to.)

Do you have any unhelpful thinking habits? List them here (check back to Chapter 11 if you need to):

List here the 7 or 8 most useful things you've learned from reading this book:

If you had to choose one main useful thing you've taken out of the book, what would it be?

Your 'Personal Action Plan'

This is your overall plan of action. Why? Because there is no point in reading a book like this, working out your 'Big Picture' and then quietly closing the book, and thinking how interesting it all has been, but not taking anything forward from today.

We may be nearing the end of the book, but for you, this is just the beginning. I want you to take action now. Now and in the next few weeks and months, or however long it needs to take. I also want you to look back over the book every so often to monitor some of the main things you've discovered or worked out on this journey.

So now, take whatever time you need, and look back over your 'Big Picture', and any chapters that you need reminding about. From this, take your time and make up your 'Personal Action Plan'. As before, this can require a bit of thinking!

All that remains to say now is that I hope you've found this a useful and helpful book, and I wish you great success in establishing your identity, rebuilding your confidence, moving forward and enjoying your life more by making your sensitivity work for you.

Below and on pages 110–11 is a template for your 'Personal Action Plan', ready to complete. Look back over the book and your 'Big Picture', and complete the Plan as best you can.

PERSONAL ACTION PLAN

Describe here in detail what you want to be doing with your life in six months' time:

How do you want to be feeling?

Describe here in detail what you want to be doing with your life in a year's time:

How do you want to be feeling?

Describe here in detail what you want to be doing with your life in two years' time:

How do you want to be feeling?

Now, look back over the book and your Big Picture, and list here all the changes in your everyday thinking you want to make, along with when to start on each change. Remember to make just one change at a time.

Change   *When*

Now, look back over the book and your Big Picture, and list here all the actions or changes (large and small) you want to make in your life, along with when you hope to do this. Remember to make just one change at a time.

Action or change
(most important first)   *When*

Useful resources

Here are some useful addresses of national organizations (many have local contacts or groups, or have distance-learning courses or support available).

Alice Muir Life Coaching
Mains of Lochridge
Stewarton
Kilmarnock
Ayrshire KA3 5LH
Tel: 01560 486888
E-mail: stresscourses@lineone.net
Website: www.stress-confidence.com

Association for Post Natal Illness
145 Dawes Road
Fulham
London SW6 7EB
Helpline: 020 7386 0868
E-mail: info@apni.org
Website: www.apni.org

British Association for Counselling and Psychotherapy
BACP House
35–37 Albert Street
Rugby
Warwickshire CV21 2SG
Tel: 0870 443 5252
E-mail: bacp@bacp.co.uk
Website: www.bacp.co.uk

Child Bereavement Trust
Aston House
West Wycombe
High Wycombe
Bucks HP14 3AG
Tel: 0845 357 1000
E-mail: enquiries@childbereavement.org.uk
Website: www.childbereavement.org.uk

Childline 0800 1111
Website: www.childline.org.uk

Cruse Bereavement Care
Cruse House
126 Sheen Road
Richmond
Surrey TW9 1UR
Helpline: 0870 167 1677
E-mail: helpline@crusebereavementcare.org.uk
Website: www.crusebereavementcare.org.uk

Depression Alliance
212 Spitfire Studios
63–71 Collier Street
London N1 9BE
Helpline: 0845 123 23 20
E-mail: information@depressionalliance.org
Website: www.depressionalliance.org

Drinkline 0800 917 8282
Website: www.patient.co.uk/showdoc/26738981

Health and Safety Executive Information Services
Caerphilly Park
Caerphilly CF83 3GG
HSE Infoline 0845 345 0055
Website: www.hse.gov.uk
Provides up-to-date books, press releases, leaflets, etc. and resources
to download free.

International Stress Management Association UK
PO Box 26
South Petherton
Somerset TA13 5WY
Tel: 07000 780430
E-mail: stress@isma.org.uk
Website: www.isma.org.uk

Mind Publications
15–19 Broadway
London E15 4BQ
Mindinfoline: 0845 766 0163
E-mail: contact@mind.org.uk
Website: www.mind.org.uk
Full catalogue of useful books, leaflets and order form available.

National Association for Premenstrual Syndrome
41 Old Road
East Peckham
Kent TN12 5AP
Helpline: 0870 777 2177
E-mail: contact@pms.org.uk
Website: www.pms.org.uk

National Drugs Helpline 0800 776600
Website: www.urban75.com/Drugs/helpline.html

No Panic
93 Brands Farm Way
Randlay
Telford
Shropshire TF3 2JQ
Helpline: 0808 808 0545
E-mail: ceo@nopanic.org.uk
Website: www.nopanic.org.uk

Parentline Plus Helpline 0808 800 2222
Website: www.parentline plus.org.uk

Relate (National Marriage Guidance)
Herbert Gray College
Little Church Street
Rugby
Warwickshire CV21 3AP
Helpline: 0845 456 1310
Website: www.relate.org.uk

Relaxation for Living Trust
168–170 Oatlands Drive
Weybridge
Surrey KT13 9ET
Produces cassettes, leaflets, etc.

Samaritans
National Helpline 08457 90 90 90
Or see local telephone directory
Website: www.samaritans.org.uk

Scottish Association for Mental Health
Cumbrae House
15 Carlton Court
Glasgow G5 9JP
Tel: 0141 568 7000
E-mail: enquire@samh.org.uk
Website: www.samh.org.uk

Stillbirth and Neonatal Death Society
28 Portland Place
London W1B 1LY
Helpline: 020 7436 5881
E-mail: helpline@uk-sands.org
Website: www.uk-sands.org

Stress Education Services
Mains of Lochridge
Stewarton
Kilmarnock
Ayrshire KA3 5LH
Tel: 01560 486888
E-mail: stresscourses@lineone.net
Website: www.stresstrain.co.uk
Provides CDs, distance-learning courses and coaching.

Turning Point
New Loom House
101 Backchurch Lane
London E1 1LU
Helpline: 020 7702 2300
E-mail: info@turning-point.co.uk
Website: www.turning-point.co.uk

Victim Support
Cranmer House
39 Brixton Road
London SW9 6DZ
Tel: 020 7735 9166
Email: contact@victimsupport.org.uk
Website: www.victimsupport.org

Women's Aid Federation
PO Box 391
Bristol BS99 7WS
Helpline: 0808 2000 247
Email: info@womensaid.org.uk
Website: womensnaid.org.uk

Workplace Bullying Advice Line
Website: www.bullyonline.org/workbully/workbully/worbal.htm

Index